How to Have a

REAL CHRISTIAN HOME

By Dr. John R. Rice

Sword of the Lord Publishers
Murfreesboro, Tennessee 37130

ISBN 0-87398-379-3

Printed and bound in the U.S.A.

Dedicated to. . . . . .

Mrs. Grace Rice MacMullen, my first-born and precious. A musician, writer, chairman of Sword Women's Jubilee, Editor Joyful Woman, delightful Christian.

Table of Contents

Father, Mother, Home and Heaven

(Sermon preached at Chicago citywide Life Begins Revival campaign, Thursday night, May 23rd, 1946. Mechanically recorded for THE SWORD OF THE LORD.)

The text is in Joshua, chapter 24. Joshua called the elders of Israel together, the heads of tribes and families, and officers and said:

"Now therefore fear the Lord, and serve him in sincerity and in truth: and put away the gods which your fathers served on the other side of the flood, and in Egypt; and serve ye the Lord. And if it seem evil unto you to serve the Lord, choose you this day whom ye will serve; whether the gods which your fathers served that were on the other side of the flood, or the gods of the Amorites, in whose land ye dwell: but as for me and my house, we will serve the Lord."

Joshua said, 'You men choose for yourselves, choose for your families; but as for me and my house, we will serve the Lord. Choose ye this day whom you will serve, but as for me and my house, we will serve the Lord.' This man speaks for his family and says, "We will serve the Lord."

I thank God we are in families. Dr. Ironside, aren't you glad you weren't just hatched out and in two weeks were scratching for your own worms! Aren't you glad that God put you in a family, and that you had a mother and a dad and brothers and sisters? In Psalm 68 the Scripture says this blessed thing, "God setteth the solitary in families."

God puts people in families as a special blessing. I think I miss my family more; I am away from them so much. It sure is good when I can get home. Not long ago somebody said, "Wouldn't you like to take off a month and go through the Rocky Mountains, spending a few days in the Garden of the Gods and the parks, and seeing the great mountains, Grand Canyon, then go through the Northwest? Wouldn't you like to take a month for that?"

"No, I wouldn't," I said.

"Why not?"

I said, "I have already seen the Rocky Mountains and Carlsbad Cavern; I have already seen the Grand Canyon and Santa Catalina Island; I have already seen the Statue of Liberty and the Battery and Mount Vernon and Betsy Ross' House. I have already seen the Smokies and the Blue Ridge mountains. I have seen Washington with the cherry trees in blossom. No, for a vacation, let me go home and eat my wife's cooking and play and sing with my children. Let me go home where I can sit in my own study and read the books I never get time for." It is a wonderful thing to me to have a home.

I am distressed that that sweet, popular song, *"Home, Sweet Home,"* is getting out of use and many people do not remember the words any more:

'Mid pleasures and palaces, though we may roam,
Be it ever so humble, there's no place like home.
A charm from the skies seems to hallow us there
Which, seek through the world, is not met with elsewhere.

Home, home, sweet, sweet home.
Be it ever so humble
There's no place like home.

Home is a blessing of God. This is a matter of sentiment, but it is not wrong to be sentimental. Something is wrong with a man who does not have any sentiment clustered around the name of mother or wife or baby. Oh, the dimpled hands of babies, the lovelight in the eyes of a good wife, the comforts of home, and the joy of the family altar! If you are not interested in that, I do not think much of either your humanity or your religion. So I come tonight to preach on the home.

I. A Christian Home Must Start With a Man

Now in a Bible kind of home we need to begin with a man. I am not sacreligious, neither do I have the cart before the horse. I am beginning where the Bible begins. I would not take one word from all the eulogy that goes properly to a good mother. Oh, the memory of my *lovely mother!* who went to be with her Lord before I was six years old. Every memory of her is a benediction. My mother taught me about the Lord. She used to get the hymnbook down in the little home, a preacher's home that was too poor to have a cottage organ; and she sang, "In the Sweet Bye and Bye," "No, Not One," "Turned Away From the Beautiful Gate," and other songs that I remember when I was four years old or so.

I remember I told a lie when I was five years old, and how she told me how God hated a lie. I think I became an accountable sinner that day. When my mother was on her deathbed she had us come to tell her goodbye and to promise to meet her in Heaven. She had my cousin sing, "How firm a foundation, ye saints of the Lord." She clapped her thin, frail hands and rejoiced, then she said, "I can see Jesus and my baby now," and smiled and fell asleep.

Her thin, transparent hands were folded across her breast and a long braid of black hair lay on her pillow. Though I was only a five-year-old boy, I remember that scene well. Yes, I devoutly thank God for every memory of my mother. We have a Mother's Day and we write verses to Mother; that is all well and good. But

God intended that a Bible home should start with a Bible kind of a man.

Joshua said, 'As for me and my house, we will serve the Lord. I'll do my part and see that the rest of them do their part.' God intended a man to lead the home for God. Always that is God's plan. God has good work for a mother, but every preacher here has experiences by the score he could call to mind of godly women, heartbroken women, who stumble along the best they can with handicaps that are unsurmountable because they have husbands who are ungodly. They cannot make their home all it ought to be because they do not have the leadership of a Christian man in the home. I say, God's plan is for a man to lead in the home.

Joshua said, 'All right, Lord, I will do it. I will decide for myself and my family.'

"Wait a minute, Joshua, wait a minute. You have grown sons, sons who are married and grandchildren and most likely great-grandchildren." (I remind you that Joshua was the next to the oldest man in the nation at this time.) I say, "Old fellow, aren't you a little quick on the trigger? How do you know you can speak for your boys and your daughters and your grandchildren? How do you know you can speak for all your servants? What about your wife? Doesn't she have a mind of her own?"

Joshua turns to me with the cold glance with which he had subdued the whole land as the major general of the army for these years past and says, 'Never mind, John, I'll attend to my family—my wife, my sons, my daughters, my servants, "As for me and my house, we will serve the Lord." I'll take responsibility for my house.'

God's way, God's plan is a man at the head. A man is 'somebody come.' Did you know that?

In the first place, man is in the image of God the Father to his children.

A man is almost a worshipful being to his children and, I say it reverently, he ought to be. When Jesus wanted to tell the converts—those who had been saved by the blood, those who loved Him, those He wanted to be formed in His image—how to pray to God and how they should feel toward Him, He said, "When you pray, say, Our Father. . . ." He said, "Like as a father pitieth his children, so the Lord pitieth them that fear him" (Ps. 103:13). He said, "Ye have not received the spirit of bondage again to fear; but ye have received the Spirit of adoption, whereby we cry, Abba, Father" (Rom. 8:15). God said, 'I will be a Father to My people. I will be a Father to those who are saved.'

Every father then should remember, "I am the image of God to my children. I'm somebody in my home. I represent Almighty God." Man is the deputy of God Almighty in the home in a very peculiar sense.

And that is not all. Man to his wife represents Christ.

In Ephesians 5:22-24, the Scripture says wives are to be in subjection to their own husbands "as unto the Lord"; that is, as if he were Jesus Christ, "For the husband is the head of the wife, even as Christ is the head of the church; and he is the saviour of the body." Christ is the Saviour of His mystical body, the church, and is the head of His mystical body, the church. I speak now softly—I tread on holy ground;—I do not understand it all, but God seems here to imply and to teach that a husband is to his wife in some sense like Christ is to the church, the head of it; and that like Christ is the Saviour, Provider and Protector for the body, the church, so the husband is to the wife the physical provider and protector for his own wife.

You see, every man who has a home represents Jesus Christ to his wife. That is why a woman is commanded to be in subjection to her husband. Here is the plain Scripture—it sounds shocking and seems as if it almost goes too far to expect this kind of an attitude toward a poor, frail, sinning, mortal man on the part of the wife—'Wives, be in subjection to your husbands, as unto the

Lord'—as if he were Christ the Lord, because the husband is to the wife an image and a reminder and, in some sense, a deputy of Jesus Christ. I say it again: Man is somebody!

No man here ever has a right to be married and take holy vows if he does not say, "By God's grace I will walk straight and be God's deputy, God's man; I'll be in the image of Christ the best I can in my home." Weak and frail as we are, a man must mean that, or he wickedly takes vows that he cannot well mean, if he does not mean to represent Christ in the home.

So you see that a man is somebody! No man ever has a right to have a home and to bring little children into this world unless he is to be to them in some measure like God, for as the little child looks up and says, "Father," so we are to look up to our Heavenly Father, God, and call Him "Father." A man is somebody!

I want you to see this truth which God makes clear in the Scripture, that a man is head of the home and the key of the success of home life.

A man should say, "If my marriage goes on the rocks, I am to blame." I know there are two sides to every question, but when it comes to responsibility for the home, the big side is the man's side. Many times a Christian woman cannot win her unsaved husband. What preacher here has found a case where a godly husband, living right and taking his responsibility, could not win his wife? There may be a few such cases, not many. God intended that men should take the lead and responsibility and the principal burden in the home for Christ. Joshua said, 'I'll take it, Lord. As for me and my house, we will serve the Lord.' God wants some good men to lead in the home, to be God's deputies, to have godly homes. So Joshua said, 'I'll take that burden.'

I hope many men here tonight will say, "If Joshua was right to say it, I ought to say it. If he ought to do it, I ought to do it. If he did it, I will try."

And it goes farther than that. Man is to be an example to his whole family.

You know there has been a wicked, hellish, ungodly, satanic teaching that by nature men are not as good as women, that by nature women are just a little better, that they are a little more naturally inclined toward God and morality and sweetness and purity of life. Don't you believe it! Not a word of Scripture bears it out. Nearly every kind of a tom-fool idea that ever got credence in this country was started by some preacher. I heard a preacher say that there was not a man in the world good enough to be the husband of a nice, pure, good and sweet woman. I say that is a lie out of Hell. I know men who are as good as any woman in the way they talk, in the way they live, in the way they pray, and in their devotion to God and their purity and holiness. There are lots of men who are just as concerned about purity and holiness and just as blameless in heart and life as any woman is. Not a line in the Bible indicates that by nature a man shouldn't be required to be as godly as any woman, as pure in his mind as any woman, as loving and kindly as any woman.

There are stronger qualities a man must necessarily carry. There are feminine attributes, and there are masculine attributes, but I will tell you frankly that holiness and purity are not feminine attributes any more than they are naturally the attributes of a man. God intended that man should set the example, lead the pace.

If you are a man who says, "I'm a man; therefore, it is all right for me to drink and not all right for my wife to drink," you are a hypocrite and are serving the Devil. Not only is the double standard in morals wrong, but it is unworkable. We thought that we would have two standards: one for the women and one for the men. We said, "You women stay on a pedestal. You are the pure ones now and you must uphold civilization."

The women said, "It's lonesome up here: we'll come down where you men are."

There was a time when if there were young men who went to the dogs, young men who went out into the sins of sex and lewdness, they went to the redlight district and only a very few women in town were ever led into sex sin. But that day is gone! These days if a man commits adultery, he does it with a woman in the same stratum of life he lives in; a boy goes with the high school girl in his own class, the kind he is going to marry, and leads her into sin. You cannot properly set one standard for men in morality and another for women. The Bible does not do anything like that, and God will put up with none of it. Every man is commanded to live as clean and pure as he expects his wife and his own children to live. That is God's plan.

When God sent the first little baby girl into my house, I held her in my hands and thought, "O God, how I need to watch my step! I must lead this little soul for eternity and God." I feel it now as I felt it then—I must live like I want my girls to live. And God is my witness, I try to do it.

A man must be an example then. Some man here tonight smokes cigarettes, yet you think it surely would be bad for a woman to smoke. I do, too. I think it is a terrible thing for a woman to smoke cigarettes. It seems to me that if a woman smokes cigarettes, she just cannot be a gentleman about it. If a woman is going to smoke cigarettes, she kind of blows smoke in your face, then she seems to say, figuratively speaking, "Now, what are you going to do about it?"

I say, I think it is bad for a woman to smoke cigarettes. I do not like it at all. Mr. Sheriff, how would you like, every time you kiss your wife, to smell a Camel! Well, I would not like it. I am not going to have any woman at my table, serving my meals and managing my household, smoking cigarettes. I am not going to have any of my daughters living at my house and smoking cigarettes. I despise it! I think it is terrible! I think it is nearly as bad for a man. But no worse! Certainly, no worse!

Listen to me, any man who has one standard for himself in moral matters and religious matters, and has a higher standard for his wife, is a hypocrite. He does not live like he talks. He does not mean business. If you are a man who does not want your little girls to smoke, nor your boys to smoke, and you smoke, you mark what I say (and if you do not believe it, I can soon prove it in private conversation), you are not sincere, you are not honest, you do not live like you talk. I say, you are a hypocrite. Your children may love you; they do not respect you. They will not respect you; no, they will not.

God said He wants man to lead the way, and Joshua said, 'I'll do it, Lord. As for me and my house, we will serve the Lord. I'll serve the Lord, then I'll see that my wife does; I'll see that my children do; I'll see that my servants do; but I will serve the Lord first. As for me and my house, we will serve the Lord.'

God wants it that way. Who should be the one to lead out in the matter of the worship in the home, in seeing that the family goes to church, and seeing that the tithes and offerings are given? Who should see that the discipline is godly and scriptural in the home? Who should lead out to see that the family understands the Bible, loves it, follows it? The husband and father should!

All over the country women want to know the answer to Bible questions. They want to know the meaning of the seven heads and the ten horns on the beast in Daniel and in Revelation; they want to know whether the Antichrist will be a Jew or whether he will be a Gentile, and many other things. The Scriptures foresaw that we poor preachers would be in a predicament. If I can help anybody out of real trouble, all right, I'd like to do that. But the Bible said, 'You women quit raising trouble in the churches. If you want to know something, you wait until you get home and ask your own husband.' That is what I Corinthians 14, verses 34 and 35 say. I'm not joking! I do not want you to laugh at that. God intended every husband and father to know more Bible than his wife and children. Any man who does not has slacked; he has shirked; he has quit on God. He is not fit to be the deputy and the high priest of his home. God intends every man to lead the way in godliness and in Bible knowledge and in a godly example. That is God's plan.

Joshua said, 'I'll do it, Lord; by Your grace, I'll do it and I'll see that my family follows me then. As for me and my house, we will serve the Lord.' Oh, God give us the right kind of men for that.

Let me tell you how this truth won an infidel.

I was in revival services in the little town of Duke, Oklahoma, a good many years ago. One pastor was concerned and he enlisted another. So we built a tabernacle, put on a roof and put tent curtains all around and put in four big coal stoves in mid-winter and heated it up, and, my, the people came! The tabernacle held twice as many as all the population of the town. It took many from the county to fill it, but they did, night after night, and we had a blessed time.

One night a man came in rather shyly. He looked a little like a Baptist deacon or a Methodist steward or a Presbyterian elder. His hair was slicked down and his face was scrubbed so it shone so red and fine, and he was all neatly dressed. He and his wife came in back yonder, looked around rather timidly and sat down next to the door. That night he liked it pretty well because I was bearing down on church members. So the next night he came halfway down the aisle and sat there. That night he chuckled a good deal at some things and looked serious at others. He liked it, so he came the next night. Right down to the front and to the second seat he came and sat.

That night I was preaching on a Christian home and I got very much interested and was not tied down to these microphones—excuse me, I am glad to have them but they kind of hinder my style—so I got down and stood on the front seat and preached. I said, "Any man who leaves it to his wife to do the praying, leaves it to his wife to take the children to Sunday school, leaves it to his wife to have prayer at the table, leaves his wife all the devotions and the godliness and trying to keep the children out of

Hell; anybody who does that, I say, is a slacker and a shirker and a quitter, and he isn't fit to have a good home."

This man whom I supposed was a Baptist deacon or a Methodist steward sat looking up at me open-mouthed, and with an innocent gaze. I looked down at him and thought, I'll prove it by this supposed deacon or steward. So I said, "Isn't that so, brother? Isn't that so? Any man who leaves it to his wife to take the children to Sunday school, leaves it to his wife to whip them and make them mind, leaves it to his wife to teach them Bible verses and try to win them to Christ, leaves it to his wife to have thanks at the table, is a shirker and slacker and a quitter and hasn't any right to have a home. Isn't that right, friend?"

He said, "Oh, ah, uh—."

I said, "Come on, isn't that true?"

He said, "I—I—I guess so."

I said, "You don't guess anything about it. You know that is so, don't you?"

He said, "Yes, I know so."

I went on with the service. That night after the service was over and we had some people saved, the Methodist pastor came to me wringing his hands. (I know I am a plague to preachers. I don't know why, but they are always afraid I am going to overturn the apple cart some way!) This good man said, "Brother Rice, you ruined it tonight. You just ruined it."

I said, "Ruined what?"

He said, "You know, that man up there on the front seat is an infidel. He has never been to hear any preacher in this town over twice, and he has been here the third night in succession and you get down there and point your finger in his face and publicly embarrass him."

I said, "I thought maybe he was a church leader. He was so interested and dressed up so nice and his hair was all slicked down."

"No, he is an old infidel and goes up and down the country

talking against the Bible and God and never comes to hear us preachers and never comes to revival services. Here he has come the third time in succession and now he is gone and will never come back."

I said, "I don't care. He admitted I was right. I got him where the wool was short that time. I shot him with both barrels one time, if I never get another whack at him."

But you know, the next night he came back, looked in the door. Nobody hit him with anything, so he walked in. He hesitated, then finally got his wife by the arm and just yanked her on down and came right down to that second seat again, and so he sat there. That was Saturday night. I do not know what I preached on that night, but again when I gave the invitation and asked people to come to Christ, I stepped down on the front seat. There he was in front of me as I stood there. I leaned over and I said, "Listen, you didn't hold your hand as a Christian."

"No, I'm not."

"Well, aren't you sick and tired of this business? Your hair is gray. You have no business going on without God. Aren't you sick and tired of your sins and going on without God?"

He said, "Preacher, to tell the truth, I am."

And I said, "Why don't you tell it to the Lord and let Him save you?"

"If I knew He would take me, I would do it in a minute," he said.

"Well," I said, "He sure will. Let me show you what He said."

I showed him some Scriptures. The song leader was going on with the singing during the invitation, but I stopped and talked with this man. I said, "What about it now?"

He said, "If I knew—."

I said, "Don't say that any more. If you want Jesus, He wants you. He will have you. Will you take Him?"

He said, "Well, if He will take me, I will."

I said, "Give me your hand on it." And he did. This was done privately between him and me and nobody else knew. The song went on. I said, "All right, you trust Him. Do you believe He saves you?"

"Yes, sir," he said, "I do."

"Well, what about coming out here now and letting this crowd know that you have turned your back on your sin and have trusted Christ to save you? What about that?"

"Preacher," he said, "listen. Would it be all right if I didn't tell anybody about this until tomorrow? For twenty years my wife has been getting up on Sunday morning, waking up the children and getting them ready and off to church while I sat around and run down the preachers and read the Sunday papers. I didn't help a bit. I've been doing that for twenty years. Listen, Preacher, wouldn't it be all right if I didn't tell anybody, didn't say a word, but just tomorrow morning get up with my family and go up to the First Christian Church where my wife has been going all these years and praying for me, and there claim Him openly? What do you think about that?"

I never told anybody in my life before or since that it would be all right to wait, but I told him it would be all right to wait until the next day to make his confession.

So the next morning he got out of bed and said, "Hey, boys, roll out. Everybody's going to church today." What in the world has happened to the old man? Everybody got ready that day to go to church. He fixed himself up fine and they all went. His wife was all tremulous, thinking it too good to be true. The children were all wondering. They all went to church. That morning he made an open confession of Christ as Saviour and since he went to the First Christian Church, they got him baptized before dinner! I do not mind if they did. That night he came down to the tabernacle and said to me, "You know, Brother Rice, I never was as much of an infidel as I thought I was."

Listen to me now. Any man who does not take the Lord has no

right to marry, has no right to a home, no right to a wife and children. It is wrong, it is sinful and weak, it is not man's part unless you say, "I'm going to take the leadership for God in my home." That is right. That is the reason the Lord said, "Likewise, ye husbands, dwell with them according to knowledge, giving honour to the wife, as unto the weaker vessel, and as being heirs together of the grace of life; that your prayers be not hindered." God help you men to be Joshuas tonight and take Joshua's vow and set out to lead your families to God. A man is somebody come if he follows God's plan. I hope you will.

II. The Wife to Be Ruled by Husband

What about the wife and mother? I cannot take much time for that just now. But I will read in Genesis 3:16. Here is a simple Scripture. May God speak to our hearts. When God is talking to parents and children about their duties to God, He speaks to parents first, but when He is talking to parents and to children about their duties to each other, He says, "Children, obey your parents in the Lord: for this is right. . .And, ye fathers, provoke not your children to wrath" (Eph. 6:1,4). If He speaks to masters and servants about their duties to each other, He says first, "Servants—" and then "Ye masters" (Eph. 6:5,9). If it is between rulers and citizens about their duty to God, it is the ruler first, but if it is their duty to each other, it is first to the one who is subject and then to the one who rules. If it is to husband and wife and their duty to God, it is the man first: like Joshua said, 'I'll serve the Lord, and my family.' But if it is duty to each other, it is wives first, then it is husbands. So it is in this case here.

Genesis 3:16 says: "Unto the woman he said, I will greatly multiply thy sorrow and thy conception; in sorrow thou shalt bring forth children; and thy desire shall be to thy husband, and he shall rule over thee." "Thy husband shall rule over thee." There it is in the Bible. Somebody says, "I don't want anybody ruling over me." Well, you are not alone. Who does? Nobody. You know, here I have been in Chicago many times and they haven't yet made me mayor. What a pity! Well, everybody cannot be mayor. Somebody has to be the rest of us, you know, to pay the bills. So it is in every church. You cannot have everybody pastor. So it is in every home. You cannot have everybody the head. God says that a wife is to be subject to her husband and her husband is to rule over her. That is God's plan. As soon as sin came in they had to have authority. As soon as sin came in they had to have somebody to obey, somebody to be subject to. So wives, this Scripture says your husbands are to rule over you. That is God's plan.

Well, you say, that is in the Old Testament. Yes, but the same God who wrote the Old Testament wrote the New, so I will read from the New Testament. In Ephesians, chapter 5, beginning with verse 22:

"Wives, submit yourselves unto your own husbands, as unto the Lord. For the husband is the head of the wife, even as Christ is the head of the church: and he is the saviour of the body. Therefore as the church is subject unto Christ, so let the wives be to their own husbands in every thing."

In what? "In everything!" You say, "My, I'm afraid that would lead a person into sin." No, do not be afraid of the Bible. You say, "Don't you think every wife ought to put God first?" Yes, that is right; but duties do not conflict. If the Bible says it, just take it. It will turn out all right. It will not lead you against what God says. You can trust it.

Somebody says, "Brother Rice, my husband is not even a Christian; my husband isn't even saved." The Lord knew all about that, so He wrote in a verse specially for you, too. Over in I Peter 3:1,2 we read:

"Likewise, ye wives, be in subjection to your own husbands [aren't you glad not to somebody else's husband, just the one you

picked out yourself]; *that, if any obey not the word, they also may without the word be won by the conversation of the wives* [let us say godly living or the habit of life of the wife]; *While they behold your chaste conversation coupled with fear.*"

But you say, "Brother Rice, I am a much better Christian than my husband." Fine! Then there ought to be no trouble at all for you to do what God says about this. If you are a good Christian, you go ahead and do what God says.

Listen to me, Christian women! How do you expect to have the favor of God? How do you expect to get your prayers answered? In the same chapter the Scripture continues, in verse 7, ". . . that your prayers be not hindered." You say, "Well I do not want to obey my husband." You wait until your baby is dying and you try to pray and God will not hear you. You wait until your boy is overseas and missing in action and you cannot hear any news, then when you try to pray God stuffs cotton in His ears and will not hear you. We had better come back to God's plan for the home. God's plan is that wives are to be subject to husbands.

"Well, Brother Rice, that would be a miserable existence," you say. Do you believe that obedience to the law, that obedience to authorities is a miserable existence? No, no, it is the lawless one who is miserable. Now let us say, "I am going to do what God said." If you are going to be a Christian, then say, "I will be happy to do what God said." He can turn it out right if you act in faith. If you trust in Him, He will do it. He said He would.

III. Godly Discipline in the Home

Let us see what the Bible says about discipline. Let me say to my preacher brethren, I know I am a very poor and awkward hand at revivals. I do not know any shortcuts to a revival. I do not know how to have a revival without penitence and without heartsearching and without holy vows and without God's people being humbled and seeking God's face. I do not want any short-cuts, I do not want any easy way—I want the old-fashioned Bible way. If you hear me tonight like you ought to, it will be easier to have a revival twenty years from now. May God give us hearts now to do right about this.

So let us see about discipline in the home. There is no discipline much anywhere these days, but turn to Proverbs, chapter 13. There is much about it in the Bible, even in the New Testament. But let me read a few verses here. Proverbs 13, verse 24:

"He that spareth his rod hateth his son: but he that loveth him chasteneth him betimes."

Somebody says, "I just love my boy too much to whip him." No you do not. You love your ease. You have no conscience, no integrity, no character, no convictions. You want your own easy, pleasant way. You do not have the character and conviction to do what God said. No, you do not love your son. "He that spareth his rod hateth his son," the Bible says, "but he that loveth him chasteneth him betimes," that is, he whips him pretty often. That is right. That is God's plan.

I turn further and we read in the nineteenth chapter of Proverbs, verse 18:

"Chasten thy son while there is hope, and let not thy soul spare for his crying."

You whip him in time. Any of you can rear your boy to turn out well if you begin in time. Now I do not know how soon you ought to begin to whip your child. I had a friend down in Texas, B. B. Crimm, an evangelist, who said, "I don't believe you ought to begin whipping girls as soon as boys. I do not believe that boys and girls are alike. For my part, I do not think you ought to begin on a girl baby until she is at least three weeks old! You can begin to whip boy babies as soon as they are born." I do not know about that, but if you do not begin to expect obedience before that little one is a year old, if you do not make him hush crying when you tell him to, you have heartbreak ahead. You sure have! "Chasten thy son while there is hope, and let not thy soul spare for his crying." That means do not quit just because he hollers a little.

I know how some of you do it. You get so mad afterwhile you grit you teeth and give the little fellow a couple of spats, then when he yells bloody murder, you have to buy him three ice cream cones and pet him half an hour to get him to shut up! But the Bible says, "Let not thy soul spare for his crying." Do not quit because he hollers; it will not kill him. He will holler like it, but it won't. It will be good for him.

I do not say that this is the way everybody ought to do it, but my dad had a rule and his rule was to whip until they cry, then whip until they stop. Well, you say, sometimes they can't stop. If my dad was whipping, they could! I know by experience! You had better take this seriously: God's plan involves that the man in the home and the woman in the home be the representatives of Almighty God and as such they must be for righteousness and they must punish sin.

I read on, Proverbs 20, verse 30:

"The blueness of a wound cleanseth away evil: so do stripes the inward parts of the belly."

You say, "Well, Brother Rice, I think I'll have him stand in the corner." Maybe that is all right in its place, but nothing takes the place of God's way. The Scripture says in the New Testament, 'Bring them up in the nurture and admonition of the Lord.' I was surprised to find that the word here that I expected to mean godly teaching, "nurture," meant chastisement. It is the same Greek word that speaks about Christ when He was scourged and is often used for chastisement in other Scriptures. I want you to know that God's Word plans for a man and woman who are starting a home to say, "We will stand for God in the home and we will see that the children stand for God, too."

I never will forget the first time I whipped one of my little girls until there were marks on her body. On a certain day she was stubborn. You know, everybody in the world sets out to spoil the preacher's children and then blame the preacher for it. She was stubborn, and after I had given her a few spanks and didn't get results, I said, "Now, Lord, You will have to help me." I waded in to get results and I spanked on the place the Lord provided for spanking little girls. Finally I saw the marks of my fingers on her little body. I went away, and I do not mind saying that I wept. I said, "Lord, I don't claim to know anything about it. I don't claim to be smart. I am just preaching the Bible. I am just taking Your Word. I am going to try and it is up to You, Lord, I am going to do what the Bible says." And with a broken heart I did it. (And I almost had to lick her mother, by the way, too!) But we got results. "The blueness of a wound cleanseth away evil: so do stripes the inward parts of the belly."

Don't you call that cruelty. You call that godliness. There is pain in the father's and mother's hearts, of course, but when it is with prayer and reverence and with godly restraint and temperance, I say sometimes nothing but stripes is going to keep a boy out of the penitentiary. Nothing but stripes will keep a girl from playing the harlot sometime. You had better listen to what God says about it.

I must hurry on. Proverbs 22:6 says:

"Train up a child in the way he should go: and when he is old, he will not depart from it."

The American Revised Version puts in another word, "and even when he is old"; when he is up and grown and out from under mother's and dad's wings and can do as he pleases, he will not leave it then, says the Word of God.

I was student pastor of a little country church in Cook county and I felt led to preach on a Christian home. After the service a man urged me to break an engagement and go with him to his home, which I did. He was agitated. When his wife had gone in the house, we stood in the front yard and he said to me, "Brother Rice, what you preached this morning isn't so."

I said, "You had better watch your step. When you say that about anything I preach, you must prove it. No man will be a member of the church of which I am pastor and challenge what I preach, unless he proves it. What do you mean?"

He said, "You said that if you rear up a child right, when he is old he will not depart from it. That isn't so."

I said, "You aren't talking about me at all. You are talking about God." I opened the Bible and said, "Here it is, read it."

He read it, then clamped his jaws and said, "All right, then the Bible isn't so. It is not so. I know I did raise my boy right."

"Where is your boy?" I asked.

"Well, I don't want to discuss that."

"You will discuss it now or you will discuss it before the church. If I am going to be pastor, you are not going to stay in the church saying the Bible isn't so. You will tell me where your boy is."

"He is in the Huntsville penitentiary for a major crime. I am not to blame. I know I did raise him right," he said.

I said, "Since you made the Bible a lie and challenged the pastor on the authority of God's Word, let me ask a question or two: Did you have a family altar at your house? Did you read the Bible, teach it to your children, have daily prayer?"

He said, "Now, wait. You city people—you may have plenty of time, but we farmers don't have any time for foolishness like that. We have got to make a living."

I said, "Then prayer and praise and Scripture in the home is foolishness and your boy is in the penitentiary and you are blaming God. Wait a minute. Let me ask you another question about this: Did you whip that boy and make him mind?" (Let me say, I was a pretty good Christian before the Lord ever found me. I mean you did not have to prove any of the things of God. When I first saw in the Bible, "Be sure your sins will find you out," I said, "Sure, I knew that a long time ago." It had already begun doing that when I found out that the Bible said sin did not pay and the wages of sin is death and the way of the transgressor is hard. My daddy had convinced me of that a long time before that. I was already on my way to being a good Christian when the Lord found me. You will understand the figurative use of the term Christian there, I hope.)

This fellow said, "Now here, my boy, you are a young man; you don't understand. When you get older you will see. My boy was high strung. You couldn't bear down on him like you could some people. He was high strung. You couldn't whip him like you can some. My boy was nervous."

I was nervous, too. I would say it with shame but that the praise of God is in my heart for what God did about it—I had such a temper that when I got angry my head would go around and I would stagger when I walked, and I had to sit down until I cooled off. I came to the point where I said, "I'll kill somebody if I don't conquer this. The thing will take me and I'll kill somebody if I don't get this temper under control." God in His mercy helped me to control it. Yes, when I was a boy I was nervous, too, but my dad just got "nervouser" than I did. That is the way to settle that.

This man said, "No, my boy was high strung, so we never whipped him." He didn't make him mind; he didn't make him get up when he called him. The boy didn't say, "Yes, Sir," to his dad and "Yes, Ma'am" to his mother. Now he is in the penitentiary and his dad is blaming God.

"One more question," I said. "Did you ever take your Bible and say, 'Son, I want you to be a Christian. We are having a revival in our church. You come on, Son, I want you to trust the Saviour. I'd like to have you come out and take Him as your Saviour openly'? Did you ever show the boy he was a sinner and that Jesus died for him? Did you teach him John 3:16 and say, 'Son, let's pray and ask Jesus to save you'? Did you ever try it?"

He said, "Now look here. I'm a Baptist, I'm not a Methodist. I never did believe in this pulling little children into the church when they didn't know anything about it."

He was such a good Baptist that he had his boy in the penitentiary, and was blaming God. You hear me. This is no joke. The Bible says that if you bring them up in the way they should go, you can stop juvenile delinquency in a really Christian home. You can have godly children coming out of really Christian homes.

Listen now to Proverbs 23:13,14:

"Withhold not correction from the child: for if thou beatest him with the rod, he shall not die. Thou shalt beat him with the rod and shalt deliver his soul from hell."

You say, "Deliver his soul from Hell?" Yes. Maybe you say, "The literal meaning is deliver his life from death." But it will deliver his soul from Hell. How could it do that? I tell you now, it is not hard to win a boy or girl to Christ who knows that sin does not pay. If he has the right kind of reverence for his dad, he is going to feel somewhat that way toward his Creator. A boy who knows, or a girl who knows, that there is authority that must be obeyed and there are judgments to face for sin and that sin does not pay—you can get that fellow or girl saved. You sure can. The right kind of rearing will keep a boy out of Hell, and when he hears the Gospel, he will turn to Christ.

God give us grace to do right in the home. He will. It will take praying, sure. It will take love, forgiveness, tears, prayers, pleadings, precepts, line upon line of it, but you can keep your children from the Devil and win them to Christ.

IV. Putting Christ First in the Home

Another word: Christ in the home, and I must hurry on. You remember when God gave the Ten Commandments from Mount

Sinai as is recorded in Deuteronomy as well as in Exodus. In the sixth chapter, verses 6 to 10, the Scripture says:

"And these words, which I command thee this day, shall be in thine heart: And thou shalt teach them diligently unto thy children, and shalt talk of them when thou sittest in thine house, and when thou walkest by the way, and when thou liest down, and when thou risest up. And thou shalt write them upon the posts of thy house, and on thy gates."

The Scripture says, "Teach them diligently unto thy children." Teach the Word of God to your children.

My youngest daughter is here tonight. She was only three when she first learned Scriptures. She said, "Children, go bey your parents in the Lord: for this is right," and she would end it triumphantly. Mrs. Rice said, "You ought to teach her not to say, 'Go bey.' Tell her to say, "Children, obey." I said, "I like that all right. She understands that." Why, any child will learn more Scripture than you have the grace to stay with them and teach them. They will take to Bible stories. My children begged me, "Daddy, tell me a Bible story." They want to know about Noah and the ark. They want to know about David and the giant. They want to know about the flood. "Daddy, tell me about John the Baptist, and about the prodigal son," and many others. They never get enough of the Bible if you begin in time. Put your heart in it. Your children will take it in. They will learn to love it and they will be molded and made into what they ought to be. Take the Word of God to your children and read it in your home. Put God first there.

And let me say a word about a family altar.

When I first married, I don't know why—perhaps because we had had it in my father's home some of the time that way—I thought, "Well, before we go to bed we will take the Bible and read a chapter or two and pray." I found that was not a good time. A pastor comes in late and an evangelist comes in late at night, tired. It is too late to ask for guidance in the day. The children were sleepy and I said, "That won't do."

So we tried it before breakfast. The hot chocolate wasn't hot, and the toast was burned and had to be scraped. Finally we planned that just as soon as breakfast is done, it's "Children, get your Bibles," and we get the Bibles for everybody around the table. These years this has been our custom and we have read through the Bible many times. I don't know how many times, I suppose fifteen times or so, through the New Testament, and five or six times through the Old Testament; the Psalms and Proverbs at least ten or twelve times. At any rate, we didn't read Ezekiel as much as we did some of the others. We have had a blessed time. If it is the Psalms, maybe we read a couple of them or three if they are shorter ones, but at least a chapter a morning. The next morning another and another and another until we read on through that book. I read two verses, then the girl to my left reads two, then the next one, and the next one, and the next one—around and back to me, then around and around the table until we read the chapter. I might say, "Mary Lloys" (who is married now), or "Grace, what is your favorite verse here?" She would tell me. Then I would say, "Elizabeth, what do you think verse 15 means?" Or I would say, "Suppose we all learn this verse." And we would. Then we would have prayer. I would pray, then we would pray around the table, each one, coming back to me and I would pray again. I got to pray three times: once before breakfast and twice after. We had a good time. When I am away the one thing I miss the most is the family worship together in the home. Listen, take time for the Bible; put it on the table.

You know at our place the girls said, "Daddy, I've got to hurry; I'll be late for school." I said, "This is more important than school. You must make sure that tomorrow morning you get up in time so we can have worship on time." So we did and we finally got it set as a pattern in our lives.

Take time for God, and then win your children to Christ.

I am glad my girls are all saved. You say, "Brother Rice, how young can a child be saved?" I don't know how young yours can be saved. Mine were all saved by the time they were about five or six years old. No, it is not a matter of smartness. But mine were carried in a basket to church by the time they were a month old and they were at Sunday school and morning worship and evening service and prayer meeting and revival. The only singing they ever heard was Gospel singing, and they learned verses of Scripture and heard us praying for revival, every last one of them, bless God. They pray for Daddy and revivals, and I am glad they do.

Oh, listen! You can win your children to Christ. Why don't you take time? Why don't you put that first? Win your children to Christ in the home. It is not hard to do, if you begin in time and mean business. God has given them into your care. Win your children while you can and God will bless you in it.

I was in southwest Texas; there was a man I so wanted to see who would not talk to me. But a baby came to that home. One day I came to the door, knocked and said, "I hear you have a new baby son, your firstborn son."

"Yes, Mr. Rice, we have," he said proudly.

"I'd like to come in and see him."

"All right, sure." And the man showed me to the mother's bedroom. She folded back the little blanket with rabbits on it, and there was the little fellow with his screwed-up eyes and his red, bald head! I looked at him and said, "Isn't he a lovely boy?" And he was—every boy is lovely. The mother, with misty eyes, looked on and hugged the little thing.

I looked down and said to her, "Now, isn't that fine? I know you are proud. Would you like for me to have a prayer that God will help you raise the baby and take good care of him and make him what he ought to be?"

"Oh, yes I would." She was so pleased about it.

I said, "All right, we will pray. Now, let's see. What do you want us to pray for? Do you want him to grow up to be a curser, a blasphemer, a drunkard and after a while die and go to Hell? Or do you want him to be a Christian and live for God and go to Heaven? Now, what shall we pray for?"

"Oh," she said, "I hadn't thought much about that. I want him to be a good man, and of course he would have to be a Christian. Yes, let's pray for him to be a good Christian man and live for God."

"All right," I said, "we will. Let's see, are you a Christian?" (I knew she was not.)

She said, "No."

I said, "Well, that's queer! How is he going to be a Christian when his mother is not a Christian? How can you teach him?" By that time she was very much distressed; her eyes were downcast and her lips quivered. I said, "Don't you think we had better pray for you, too, that you will be a Christian, so you can teach him about God and lead the way?"

"I wish you would," she said, "I certainly need it. You know I never realized how important it is for a mother to be a Christian before today."

So I said, "All right, we will pray for you, too."

Then I turned to the father and said, "What about you? Are you a Christian?"

He said, "No, I am not."

I said, "Then why is that motto on the wall?—

'Christ is the head of this house, the unseen Guest at every meal, the silent Listener to every conversation.'

"What do you have that for?"

He said, "I saw it and thought it was pretty. I thought my wife would like it, so I brought it home."

"Well, it isn't true," I said.

"No, it isn't. I guess I'll have to take it down. You know, that is just a lie, isn't it? Christ isn't the Head of this house. I will have to take it down, I guess. I thought it was so nice, but I don't have any right to that. I see that."

I said, "While I pray for the baby and for the mother, let's pray for you and let's ask Jesus to come in and be the head of the home."

He sat there in a canebottom chair with his face down in his hands, and the tears dropped between his fingers. He said, "Yes, do." His voice was colored with emotion as he said it.

I prayed, and all the angels stopped strumming on their harps and listened; the mother wept and held the little one by her side tightly; the father sat in his chair with his head bowed and the tears dripping between his fingers. I asked God to take the little baby and care for him, to help the mother and the father to be Christians so they could rear him right.

Then when we were through praying, I said to the lady, "Are you going to take Jesus as your Saviour and trust Him and live for Him?"

"Yes, I will," she said. The man did the same thing, and Christ came in to be the Head of the home.

Don't you want Him to be the Head of your home? I hope you do. Let me ask a question: How many men here tonight will take Joshua's vow? Many have taken it before. I have, too. Here in the presence of some of my family I want to do it again. I want to do it again. I want to stand up here and say like Joshua, "As for me and my house, we will serve the Lord." Don't say it unless you plan to lead the way for the family. Don't say it if you are to go on with dirty habits you do not plan for them to have. Don't you say it unless you mean yes to God's plan for you as His deputy and high priest in the home. But I hope you will say, "If God will help me, I will undertake it. I will serve God and put Him first and lead my family to God. With His help I will try." How many men would like to say it?

(First the pastors and evangelists, then hundreds of Christian men stood to take Joshua's vow, to set out to lead their families for Christ. Some men were converted. Then wives and children joined in the holy vow to make the home a Christian home.)

Will you, too, fathers and husbands who read this, take that vow today, and make your life and your home what God wants them to be?

"Home, Sweet Home"

The Dearest Place on Earth, the Nearest Place to Heaven Is a Happy Christian Home

Home can be almost a hell on earth. The week before this was written in Dallas, Texas, a man came to the home of his estranged wife with a shotgun. She pleaded in vain for her life, then turned and ran. The full charge of shot hit her in the back and she fell, dead. Then the man put the muzzle of the gun to his mouth, blew away the whole side of his face and fell mortally wounded.

Home can be almost a hell on earth.

In our nation there are about half as many divorces as there are marriages. Dissension, jealousy, suspicion or hate have turned the marital cup into gall, air castles of love into ashes. Drinking, unfaithfulness, brutality and desertion played their part in these home tragedies. And only God knows how many homes are miserable besides those dissolved in divorce.

Some couples applied for divorces and did not get them; other homes are held together only by children; some wives endure their husbands for financial support, and some husbands keep their wives to avoid scandal.

Certain it is that homes are not always happy homes. Homes can be failures, places where families endure but do not enjoy each other. Sometimes family ties are little more than a convenience. Often homes are little hells on earth.

But home was not so intended. The good God who instituted marriage and the family, provided that homes should be a blessing and joy, a refuge of peace and happiness, a haven from trouble and strife and sorrow. God intended that home should be "the dearest place on earth, the nearest place to Heaven."

The First Home, in the Garden of Eden

Little as we think about it, the institution of the home, marriage and family was meant for perfect people in a paradise of beauty! Home was intended to be the last step to perfect happiness in a lovely and sinless world.

God made Adam, the first man, perfect and holy, in His own image. Even in the Garden of Eden, God said, "It is not good that the man should be alone; I will make him an help meet for him" (Gen. 2:18). So He made a woman and brought her to the man. Adam loved her and she was his wife.

Thus God Himself in the Garden of Eden founded the first home. It was the last step needed for perfect happiness on earth in the paradise of God.

After that, the curse of sin entered in and Adam and his wife became sinners and all their descendants are cursed with the taint of sin. Every person is a poor, fallen creature. Nature itself bears the marks of the curse that came with sin. The world has become a place of war, crime, hate, and rebellion against God and unnamable wickedness and violence.

Yet when the angels with a flaming sword drove Adam and Eve from the Garden, they brought part of the paradise with them. God's loving mercy provided that the outcasts should take with them the Edenic blessing of marriage, love and home!

Every home, then, is a part of the Garden of Eden. Every home is meant to be a heaven on earth. Every home should be a refuge from a sin-cursed world all about us and a likeness of our heavenly home which God has prepared for those who love Him.

The Christian Home Depends on a Christian Marriage

Happiness in the home depends on having God there and having the home honor Christ. Only where Christ is Lord can happiness have full place. If we expect to have a little bit of Heaven in our home, then we must have Christ there, and His will must be done.

Sin brings trouble and heartache. It always has; it always will. Sin broke up the Garden of Eden. Sin has brought death into the world. Every sickness, every failure, all the trouble, misunderstanding, and heartbreak of the world has been brought in by sin.

So the only way to have a blessed home is to have a Christian home where the principals in marriage are saved people putting Christ first.

It is dangerous for a Christian to marry one who is not saved. Can Christ and Satan both be Lord in the same house? Can you mix Hell with Heaven and still make the home happy? When a Christian marries a child of Satan can one expect their union, the most intimate of all human relationships, will be a happy one? No, no! The marriage of a Christian to an unsaved person is a sin against God, and the certain result is misery and unhappiness.

I have often seen where God has answered the tearful prayers of a wife for her unsaved husband, or of a husband for his unsaved wife. Sometimes after many years prayer has been answered and the loved one, married years ago in defiance of the plain command of God (a sinful marriage it was), is saved. God's mercy is great. He is willing to forgive sin.

Yet every pastor and evangelist knows that the most frequent and heartbreaking failure of answered prayer is that of a wife praying for her husband whom she married contrary to the command of God. Many times such are never saved, or are saved after much suffering and trouble in the home. A Christian marrying an unbeliever sins against God and makes sure of trouble.

God's Word says in II Corinthians 6:14-18:

"Be ye not unequally yoked together with unbelievers: for what fellowship hath righteousness with unrighteousness? and what communion hath light with darkness? And what concord hath Christ with Belial? or what part hath he that believeth with an infidel? And what agreement hath the temple of God with idols? for ye are the temple of the living God; as God hath said, I will dwell in them, and walk in them; and I will be their God, and they shall be my people. Wherefore come out from among them, and be ye separate, saith the Lord, and touch not the unclean thing; and I will receive you, And will be a Father unto you, and ye shall be my sons and daughters, saith the Lord Almighty."

Righteousness with unrighteousness is mismated. Light mated with darkness is sin. Christ does not have concord with Belial. He that believeth should not have part with an infidel (an unbeliever). The temple of God (the Christian's body) is not at agreement with idols. Therefore the command of God is, "Come out from among them, and be ye separate, saith the Lord, and touch not the unclean" [*Thing* is not in the original. God does not mean an unclean thing, but an unclean person], "and I will receive you, And will be a Father unto you, and ye shall be my sons and daughters, saith the Lord Almighty."

If home is to be "the dearest place on earth, the nearest place to Heaven," it must be a place where there is basic harmony between husband and wife, harmony about the deepest things, the highest things, the noblest things. In other words, Christ must be ruler in both hearts or there can be no heaven in the home.

And let me say here that human love, however high and lofty, cannot guarantee happiness. Here in America we are wont to think that love is the sum of all that is necessary to make a successful marriage. Not true! We have known cases where drunkenness, nagging, brutality, incompatibility, dissension and disagreement about the holiest things in life came in where love was truly present.

An unsaved man's love for his wife will not give him a good heart. An unsaved man's love for his wife may not be able to conquer the demon of thirst for drink. An unsaved woman's love for her husband will not always make her willing to give up the habits and thoughts and plans of a lifetime. Human love is not sufficient to guarantee happiness in the home.

Do you suppose of the marriages that took place in America last year, that in one out of two cases there was no true love? But about half of the marriages are ending with divorce. That does not mean that human love was not truly present. Men and women who could not live together in peace often have told me they still loved each other. It simply means that if happiness is to reign in the home there must be something beyond carnal, human love.

Love cannot regenerate the human heart. Love does not make one Christlike. Sin abides in the heart that has only human love as a motive. And sin brings trouble anywhere it appears. Even in Heaven happiness would be spoiled if sin were admitted to work its havoc.

So home can be happy in proportion as Christ is Lord and as both husband and wife put their dependence on God, love and trust Him and put Him first in their lives. Therefore, it is folly for a Christian to marry one who is unsaved. God plainly commands, "Be ye not unequally yoked together with unbelievers."

In Rhome, Texas, some years ago, I preached on this. The next day a little woman came to me and laughingly said, "I know what you preached about last night, even when I was not here, and I do not believe it!"

"I think you surely must be mistaken. If you know what I preached, you would surely agree with it for it is in the Bible," I said. "Read this Scripture with me." So I turned to II Corinthians 6:14-18.

She read it over. Her face became grave. Before she read through the whole passage, tears flooded her eyes. Weeping, she said, "I didn't know it was in the Bible! Why didn't some preacher tell me this fifteen years ago?"

I knew what caused her tears and broken heart. She had married an unsaved man. Her fourteen-year-old son, following in the footsteps of his wicked father, was now breaking her heart. She could not get him to attend services, nor get him interested in the things of God. He preferred to follow his father. She was reaping what she sowed.

I feel my responsibility to you young people. So I beg you, if you are a Christian, do not marry an unsaved person. To do so is to sin against God. To do so means heartache. No human quality of character can guarantee a happy home. Human love cannot bring happiness. Only the blessing of God can make the home happy. For your mate, choose only one who knows the Lord Jesus and is willing to put Him first in heart and life.

Solomon, the man greatly loved of God, and to whom God gave wisdom as to no other human being, sinned in this matter. Nehemiah said, in rebuking Israelites who after the captivity had sinned by marrying into the heathen people, "Did not Solomon king of Israel sin by these things? yet among many nations was there no king like him, who was beloved of his God, and God made him king over all Israel: nevertheless even him did outlandish women cause to sin" (Neh. 13:26).

Marriage with unsaved women caused the wisest man who ever lived to sin. Such ungodly marriages bring the displeasure of God. Many times they forfeit His blessings upon the home.

If you have committed this sin, beg God to forgive you. You cannot undo your marriage, and you ought not. The Scripture commands, "If any brother hath a wife that believeth not, and she be pleased to dwell with him, let him not put her away" (I Cor. 7:12).

Divorce is not the remedy for this wrong. Two wrongs do not make a right. Any marriage, recognized by men, is now binding in the sight of God. Your sin is of the past. All you can do is to beg God to forgive you and to undo, as far as possible, the wrong and harm that have been wrought by your sin.

But to you who have not yet committed this sin, I beg you, beware! Any person who marries one of the Devil's children is certain to have trouble with his father-in-law, Satan!

No home can be happy until Christ is the Lord of the home, the King in the hearts of both man and woman. Success and happiness and peace are only relative, only a fraction of what it could be if Christ had His way in the hearts of both husband and wife.

Perhaps some wife reads this message who has an unhappy home. Your husband is unsaved. Or, less frequently, some husband will read it whose wife is unsaved. May I say to you kindly, you can never expect real spiritual happiness in your home without Christ in the hearts of those who make the home.

If your loved one is unsaved, then today do your best. Get that husband or wife to trust in Christ as Saviour. Make your home united around Jesus Christ. That is the only hope for happiness.

Or if you who read this are unsaved, you are the fly in the ointment. If you are unsaved in a home where others are Christians, then you are the serpent in the Garden of Eden. "There is no peace, saith my God, to the wicked" (Isa. 57:21). Your home cannot be fully happy without Christ. Oh, turn to Christ today and make your home happy with His presence.

Little Children Needed to Make a Happy Home

God founded the first home. A happy paradise it was! We are told, "God blessed them, and God said unto them, Be fruitful, and multiply, and replenish the earth, and subdue it" (Gen. 1:28).

Even had man not sinned, God planned that the family should have children. And after sin had brought the wreck of the whole world, and God had swept away civilization in the Flood, God repeated the same command to Noah in Genesis 9:1: "And God blessed Noah and his sons, and said unto them, Be fruitful, and multiply, and replenish the earth."

I know that there are some who cannot have children. God does not always give the blessed privilege of motherhood and fatherhood. But in Bible times, barrenness was regarded as a calamity. Hear the pleading prayer of Hannah, the long continued supplication of Sarah, Isaac interceding for his wife Rebekah, the jealous competition between Leah and Rachel, the joy of the aged Zacharias and Elisabeth when the angel promised the birth of John the Baptist. Yes, according to Bible standards, children are essential to the fullest happiness. "As arrows are in the hand of a mighty man; so are children of the youth. Happy is the man that hath his quiver full of them" (Ps. 127:4,5).

Let modern women be more concerned, if they must, about their schoolgirl complexions and their slender, lovely forms. The painting of the nails, rouge on the face, lipstick and permanent waves—these may be the highest themes of thought and ambition of many modern women. But these never did satisfy a heart nor make the home happy.

It is said that while children are little they trample upon your toes, and when they are grown, they trample upon your heart. I suppose that is true for most people. Well, let us have them trampling on our toes, and if it must be, trampling upon our hearts. But God deliver us from an old age without children! Women had better learn to fear barren lives, fruitless wombs and breasts that never gave suck.

God help me that, after all the sorrows and toil and gray hair children may bring, I may yet rejoice to hold my grandchildren and see them grown and happy and prosperous in the blessing of God, serving their fellowman and giving their testimony for Christ!

Children cost! Certainly they cost, from the heaviness of the mother and the pangs of childbirth, on down to the burdens of their adulthood. But children reared in the fear of God, saved by His grace, trained and admonished in His Word, are worth all they cost and more!

Some homes are never happy. Wives spend money and time, depending upon form and skin and clothes and hair dressing and jewels, to hold the love of husbands, when what they need is little bodies they can love and handle and train; little minds they can enlighten.

Homes would not be so easily broken if they had a real tie of flesh and blood. A man and wife whose blood has mingled in the veins of their offspring will not so quickly separate. Those who have watched beside the same little sickbed, had their prayers answered as they listened so carefully to the doctor's verdict, surely have something that will hold them together as they override many storms of a nagging tongue, neglect or abuse.

So I advise every husband and wife who can have children to do so, particularly if they are Christians who are fit to rear them.

May I say that part of the grief, sin, violence, and wickedness at the present time is to be blamed on the so-called Christian homes? The homes of the poor, the unlettered, the shiftless, continue to multiply. In the homes of well-bred, well-trained, cultivated people, children are scarce. If the men and women best fitted to be fathers and mothers have large families reared in the nurture and admonition of the Lord, our civilization would have salt enough to keep it from the destruction threatening it today.

Only eternity can tell how preachers' children have blessed the world. Why should the man who develops only his muscles have more children than the man who develops his mind and character?

Some homes can be happy if God sees fit to withhold the blessings of children. But all who can have children should do so. That home reaches its highest and fullest joy when father and mother and children together please God and give their best to Him.

Discipline and Authority in the Home

There can be no happiness without authority. The kingdom of Christ can never come on earth until His will is done here as it is in Heaven. Only when rebellion came in was man cast outside the garden, a fallen soul. No home can be happy without authority.

The basis of all sin is rebellion against authority. The reason for all the crimes against society is rebellion against authority.

We spoke at a county jail. Four hundred sixty-five men and women were there. However diverse their crimes, they were there because they rebelled against authority. Every man in the penitentiary is there for that very reason. Every person in Hell goes there primarily because he rebels against the authority of God, refuses to obey His commands, refuses to trust God's Son, refuses to surrender to His will.

We must remember that "the powers that be are ordained of God" (Rom. 13:1). God demands obedience to law, obedience to authority. In the home that must be true if you are to have the blessing of God and peace, if home is to be a little bit of heaven upon earth.

Rebellion means crime and sin, and these always bring unhappiness. For this reason God has provided that the wife should be subject to her husband. He said to Eve, just outside the Garden of Eden, "Thy desire shall be to thy husband, and he shall rule over thee." In the New Testament women were also commanded to be in subjection and under obedience to their own husbands (Eph. 5:22,23; I Pet. 3:1,6; Titus 2:5).

How necessary, then, that children be under authority!

God commended Abraham, and confided His plans to Abraham as He explained: "For I know him, that he will command his children and his household after him, and they shall keep the way of the Lord, to do justice and judgment; that the Lord may bring upon Abraham that which he hath spoken of him" (Gen. 18:19).

In the days of the baby Samuel, Eli was a devout and godly man. Yet upon him and his whole posterity came the curse of God, "because his sons made themselves vile, and he restrained them not" (I Sam. 3:13). God said that in not controlling his children, Eli "honourest thy sons above me" (I Sam. 2:29).

This duty of discipline in the home is one of the cardinal Bible doctrines. So strict was God's plan about it that a father and mother were commanded to see their son stoned if he were rebellious and would not hearken unto them (Deut. 21:18-21). Rebellion in the home is counted as one of the sins worthy of death, along with murder, rape and kidnapping!

"Honour thy father and thy mother" is one of the Ten Commandments, which compose all the law of God. Fathers and mothers were commanded to "chasten" the son, and if he were still rebellious and would not heed and became a drunkard and a glutton, a rebel, he was, under Mosaic law, to be counted an enemy of society and executed.

So important is the discipline of children that in the New Testament it is plainly forbidden that a man should be bishop or pastor of a church, if he has children accused of riot or unruly (I Tim. 3:1-5).

Again, it is required of one who is to be a pastor that he be one "having his children in subjection with all gravity; (For if a man know not how to rule his own house, how shall he take care of the church of God?)" (I Tim. 3:4,5).

Do you believe in whipping children? The Bible is very clear on that. I have dealt with this in detail in chapter 1, using such Scriptures as Proverbs 13:24; 19:18; 20:30. Oh, take this matter of discipline to heart! Doubtless, many are in Hell now because they were not punished for sin back in their early years.

Parents, as you love God and believe His Word, as you love your children and long for them to grow into good men and women, with the favor and blessing of God, then *demand obedience,* demand careful, quiet, immediate answers to questions, demand obedient action when you speak. Yes, teach your child that rebellion is as the sin of witchcraft and idolatry (I Sam. 15:23). By so teaching him now, you may have tears and heartache. You may be misunderstood. You may often despair and think you are failing. But one day, thank God, you will see the reward and will find that it pays to do what God has said.

THERE IS NO WAY TO HAVE A HAPPY HOME WITHOUT DISCIPLINE.

Proverbs 29:15 tells us why many a mother is brought to shame by her children. "The rod and reproof give wisdom: but a child left to himself bringeth his mother to shame." Again Proverbs 29:17 says, "Correct thy son, and he shall give thee rest; yea, he shall give delight unto thy soul."

Oh, the joy of well brought-up, quiet, reverent, obedient, respectful young people! Such children are easy to win to Christ. They find it easy to hold a job. They learn to study, to work, to avoid sin.

God gives us some twenty years to make men and women out of our children. Let us be careful that we do not sin by avoiding punishment. Chastening is in God's plan of raising children! The home that does not have strict discipline is not a Bible kind of home. It will not have the peace of God long upon it.

The Boy Who Killed His Mother Was Never Spanked

A few years ago the following appeared in the daily papers:

"Dad forgives boy who slew his mother"

"CHICAGO, ILL., *March 5 (UP).—Theodore Danielsen, who thought he had been bringing up a musical genius, decided today to forgive his son for killing his mother.*

"Danielsen interviewed his 16-year-old son, Theodore, Jr., in jail last night. Teddy told him that he had killed his mother with a bread knife. Father and son wept together and the father listened to the boy's story, his arms around him, his head bowed.

" 'I'm still your friend,' the father said. 'Keep your chin up. You're all I have left.'

"To police, Danielsen said:

" 'He has a very quick temper. We never spanked him.'

"Teddy played the piano well and his teachers called him an 'embryonic genius.' Mrs. Danielsen, who also played the piano well, made him practice daily.

"Teddy killed her Thursday. She was making a cherry pie in the kitchen. He came in. She learned that he hadn't been to school for two weeks. She reprimanded him and he picked up the bread knife off the table and ran it into her throat. He took $5.00 and jewelry from his mother's purse and fled. Police arrested him yesterday.

"Teddy told the police that he killed his mother because she slapped him and scratched his cheek and seemed about to slap him again."

"He has a very quick temper. WE NEVER SPANKED HIM!" That is the reason he had such a temper! *The Dallas Journal* commented editorially about this case, that here is youth left free to express himself, without restraint.

Dear friend, happiness does not come to the home that has no authority, no discipline, no restraint, no punishment of sin. If you want the peace of God to abide in your home, then husband, father, take your place as the minister of God, the head of the home, and see that righteousness prevails there.

It will take prayer, tears, pleading, and sometimes chastising. It will take a good example and earnest seeking after the right. But it is worth it, and there is no other way to have a home where God can abide in great blessing.

The Bible is never out of date, and in this matter it is as infallibly correct as it is on the plan of salvation. The home which is "the dearest place on earth, the nearest place to Heaven," is a place where there is peace and order, with a reverence and respect for authority, which, in the last analysis, means a respect for God and a surrender to His will.

Christ Must Be Put First in the Home

Homes that are like Heaven must put Christ first. He was first in the creation. He it was who met Adam and talked with him in the Garden of Eden. God has planned that in Him all things should consist and that in all things He should have the preeminence. God has committed all judgment to the Son. Jesus Himself said, "All power is given unto me in heaven and in earth" (Matt. 28:18). So, then, if you would have a happy and blessed home, put Christ first.

What part does the church have in your home? Is it counted an honor to be a church member? When you move your residence, do you immediately put your membership in a church of God's leading and choice, in the new community where you reside?

And do you regularly attend the services whenever the doors are open? Are you in your place in Sunday school, in the morning and evening preaching services on Sunday, in the prayer meeting on Wednesday night? Do you take some active part, to fulfill your ministry, your stewardship of the Gospel? If not, how could you expect God to make such a home happy?

Children will not follow the precept of a father and mother whose example does not tell the same thing. It is a pitiful thing that it should ever be necessary to say about parents, like Jesus said about the scribes and Pharisees, "Whatsoever they bid you observe, that observe and do; but do not ye after their works: for they say, and do not" (Matt. 23:3). Children will have no confidence in a hypocrite. They know whether you mean business for God.

When your children see you day by day putting business before the church, putting your pleasure before God, putting money-making before soul winning, reading other literature before reading the Bible, do you suppose they believe in the sincerity of your claims as a Christian? Do you suppose they are impressed by your devotion to God? Do you suppose they see any reason for trusting Christ and loving Him and serving Him? So, about many a parent it could honestly be said, "What you do talks so loud I cannot hear what you say!"

Put Christ first in your home if you want the peace of God to dwell there. We have it plainly said in the Word of God, "I the Lord thy God am a jealous God, visiting the iniquity of the fathers upon the children unto the third and fourth generation of them that hate me" (Exod. 20:5). You may expect your children to follow in your footsteps. You cannot expect them to love God and serve Him, to put Him first, unless you do the same.

At our home as a boy (it is one of my happy memories!) we always expected to go to church. My father, my stepmother, the whole family (too many to ride in one carriage!) went to church. We went when it was cold and when it was hot. We went when it rained and when it was dry. It was rare indeed that any were so sick they could not go. If that were true, the rest went to church, and just one stayed home to take care of the sick. We went to church and Sunday school on time. We went to prayer meeting.

I thank God for the happy memories that proved to me the sincerity of my father's faith in God.

Is Christ put first in your home? Do you have thanks at the table? Are little children taught to bow their heads and to be grateful to God for daily bread? Remember the disciples who went down to Emmaus in their sadness and were cheered with the presence of One whom they did not know. They recognized Him by the blessing of the bread! And your children can recognize Christ in you when they are accustomed to daily prayer, gratitude, to reverence in the home.

Does your home have Christian mottoes, Scripture verses on the walls? Are the children accustomed to hearing Mother and Father pray? Are they taught to lift their little voices in thanks and in petition? Are they accustomed to the Word of God as the fountain of blessing which Father and Mother have found it to be?

I beg you, put Christ in your home if you want happiness there!

Once I was in the home of a good Christian man who had just died. He said he was ready to go, and his family believed him. But they said to me, "O Brother Rice, but we never heard him pray! If we could only have heard him pray!"

Home can only be a little bit of Heaven upon earth as Christ is recognized as the Head of the home.

I am certain that even poverty and the attendant evils and sorrows of it are usually caused by our sins. The home where Christ is honored with the first-fruits of all the increase is usually a prosperous and happy home.

Every home should expect the blessing of Malachi 3:10, "Bring ye all the tithes into the storehouse, that there may be meat in mine house, and prove me now herewith, saith the Lord of hosts, if I will not open you the windows of heaven, and pour you out a blessing, that there shall not be room enough to receive it."

Remember that Jesus Himself promised, "Give, and it shall be given unto you; good measure, pressed down, and shaken together, and running over, shall men give into your bosom" (Luke 6:38).

Where want, and poverty, and stark hunger is, it is likely true that those who have sowed sparingly have reaped sparingly. Where plenty is, even a modest plenty, with the blessing of God, it is often true that 'he that sowed bountifully has reaped also bountifully' (II Cor. 9:6).

Every home can claim the promise of Jesus, "Seek ye first the kingdom of God, and his righteousness; and all these things shall be added unto you" (Matt. 6:33). Daily food can come, like manna from Heaven, to those who trust Christ, put Him first and claim His promises.

Let every home, then, make God first in money matters and expect God's blessing in money matters.

Win Children to Christ

Blessed is the father who assumes the responsibility for the salvation of his children. Such fathers have come to me many times with great rejoicing to tell me when the last child has been converted, "Brother Rice, the last one is saved! We are all in the family of God and the circle will not be broken!"

The home cannot be happy when a prodigal boy or a wayward girl breaks the heart of Mother and Father. The home cannot be happy where the children grow up and forget Mother's God and Father's God. The only sure hope for happiness through the years is that each child, as he comes to the years of accountability, be won to Christ, to love Him, to trust Him, to follow Him in baptism, to get in the church with God's people, to obey the Lord and grow in grace.

If you want the happiness in your home, win your children to Christ.

I wrote years ago about my new baby: "Just a few months ago God gave us our baby, Sarah Joy. The other five children had all been converted. We had rejoiced more than once that now all of our little ones had found peace in Christ and we would be a united family in Heaven. And now, with the joy that comes with our five-months-old baby, there comes also a heavy responsibility that we cannot shake off.

"I have just been thinking, What if we should all get to Heaven but this little one, and she be left outside! I have gotten accustomed now, with some difficulty, to speaking of 'my six little girls' where I used to speak of 'my five girls.' Wouldn't it be a sad and terrible tragedy if, when we get to Heaven, Mrs. Rice and I would have to speak again of 'our five little girls' and never mention the other, because we failed to win her to Christ?

"I thank God that He helped us with the other five, and that they each one, when they were five or six years old, were taught to trust in Christ, and did. With prayer, with tears, with deep anxiety, the other children were won to Christ.

"I will never forget how happy we were when the first one, Grace, found the Saviour. What a load lifted! Then with Mary Lloys, the second girl, in 1930 while her mother was reading to her the story of the crucifixion from Matthew, suddenly burst into tears and said, 'Mother! Mother, I want to be saved!' And when little Joanna, the last one, found Christ, not long ago, we were so happy. Now, what if the last one should grow up without any faith in her father's God, without loving Christ or trusting Him? What if she should wander away in sin and break our hearts? Home could not be happy as it ought to be with one prodigal. So, father and mother, I beg you, win your children to Christ."

Thank God, that baby girl has long been a devoted Christian. How glad I am that we have a united Christian family for earth and Heaven!

Not long ago I was reading an old Bible given me by my father. He had given me to God to be a preacher when I was a baby. I never knew about it until long afterward, after my mother was dead. I learned that she had called me repeatedly in letters to her loved ones, "My preacher boy." She had wanted me to preach the Gospel and begged God to make me a preacher.

Then when I read in my father's Bible, I found underlined the words of Zacharias on the birth of his dear son, "His name is John," and I thought, and my eyes filled with tears, that God had put it in the heart of my father that I might in some sense be a John the Baptist, a preacher in the spirit and power of Elijah, filled with the Holy Ghost, if not from my mother's womb, then at least throughout my ministry! And I wept and prayed that my father's prayers might be fulfilled and that in truth I might live up to my name! Give your children to Christ.

Will I ever forget the day that my mother went home to Heaven? I was only five, hardly six years old. We were called in from our play. In the room, gathered around my mother's bed, were my father and a number of kinspeople. All were weeping except Mother. She said to my cousin, "Georgia, won't you play and sing for me?" Cousin Georgia answered, "What shall I sing, Aunt Sadie?" My mother called for that old song which had blessed her heart so many times,

"How firm a foundation, ye saints of the Lord,
Is laid for your faith in His excellent Word!"

So Cousin Georgia played it, and tried to sing it, though she could not sing much for weeping. Then my mother called us one by one and had us promise to meet her in Heaven. When we had promised, she looked up and said, "I can see Jesus and my baby now!" Then she smiled around at us and closed her eyes and went to sleep.

Oh, the joy in our home because of the mother we had to win us to Christ! I was not saved then, but a little later I was converted, and the joy and peace of certainty of my heart on the matter of Christ and the Bible, is largely guaranteed by the testimony of my sweet mother who is in Heaven!

I thank God for a happy home. I thank Him for a wife who loves me and for children who are sweet and good. I thank God that all have trusted Christ as Saviour. I can truly say,

'Mid pleasures and palaces though we may roam,
Be it ever so humble, there's no place like home.
A charm from the skies seems to hallow us there,
Which, seek through the world, is ne'er met with elsewhere.

An exile from home, splendor dazzles in vain;
Oh! give me my lowly thatched cottage again;
The birds singing gaily, that came at my call,
Give me them, and that peace of mind dearer than all.

Home, home, sweet, sweet home.
There's no place like home,
O, there's no place like home.

And many another like John Howard Payne, the writer, who never had a home of his own, could write these words, longing for the paradise and peace hereafter which here they have been denied. If you have a home, guard it safely. Let Christ be there and have His way. But make sure of a home in Heaven.

One day we will gather in the heavenly home. Will the circle be unbroken? Are you ready to meet your mother, and your father, and all the loved ones gone on before? If not, then I beg you, get ready.

Homes down here are frail things at best. We are troubled with all the sins and failures and mistakes to which the flesh is heir. The best home has been marred by sin. Even where every member of the family is a Christian, sin comes to bring misunderstandings and trouble.

When death breaks the ties of home, we say good-bye to Mother or Father at the grave. Distance ofttimes separates the chiefest loved ones. Children grow away from parents and leave. One gray-headed companion is left to mourn alone when the other is carried to the Silent City of the Dead. An earthly home at best is but a picture of a heavenly home when God Himself shall wipe away all tears from our eyes. One day Eden will be restored!

One day we can meet our loved ones in the paradise of God! Don't you want to meet Him in peace? Don't you want to be a part of the happy home there which God prepares for them who love Him?

Oh, think of the home over there
By the side of the river of life;
Of the saints all immortal and fair
In their home in the palace of light.

Today is a fleeting day. In the Father's house of many mansions we can have a home that will never be broken by death or sorrow. Whatever your lot here, with its disappointments and failures, make sure that you have part in the home over there.

Jesus Christ is the way. Put your trust in Him today and have the peace and forgiveness and a bit of Heaven in your heart! Then when He comes for His own we will enter into the eternal rest and joy of Home, Sweet Home, with God!

The Bible on Child Correction and Discipline

The Bible Teaches That Parents Are Accountable for Conversion, Christian Character of Children and Later Life. Strict Obedience to Be Enforced by Whipping

All the trouble in the world can be traced to rebellion against authority. Satan rebelled against God. As Lucifer, the Angel of Light, he said, "For thou hast said in thine heart, I will ascend into heaven, I will exalt my throne above the stars of God. I will ascend above the heights of the clouds, I will be like the most high" (Isa. 14:13,14).

That was the beginning of all sin. Adam and Eve brought sin to the human race when they rebelled against God's authority and disobeyed His command in eating of the forbidden fruit of the tree of knowledge of good and evil (Gen. 3).

All crime is simply rebellion against the law and the authority of the government. The international crimes of Hitler and Stalin are a deliberate violation of the authority of treaties and sworn agreements between nations and the enlightened conscience of the world represented by international law.

The breakdown of modern homes resulting in the alarming increase of divorces is largely the result of the breakdown of authority in the home. Brides do not promise to obey their husbands or if they promise, they do not mean it. Husbands do not assume, and wives do not yield to the authority which God requires of husbands. There is no authority to bind the modern home together.

In ages past when people broke the Ten Commandments they still acknowledged their righteousness and force. Now, pink and red professors, modernist preachers and so-called "liberal" philosophers deny the authority of any standard of morals and sometimes teach that there is no harm in adultery, or that covetousness is laudable, that there is no God but every man's own desires or the conscience and morals of the race.

All sins result, I say, from the breakdown of authority or rebellion against authority.

Back of all unbelief in the head is rebellion in the heart. "The fool hath said *in his heart,* There is no God" (Ps. 53:1).

Unbelief in the Bible is *heart rebellion* against God. Jesus said, "O fools and *SLOW OF HEART* to believe all that the prophets have spoken" (Luke 24:25).

One who refuses to trust Christ is really guilty of heart rebellion. Faith in Christ as one's own Saviour is not simply the mental assent to certain doctrines or a creed. To believe that Christ is the Son of God who died for sinners is not saving faith. "Thou believest that there is one God; thou doest well; the devils also believe, and tremble" (James 2:19). No, saving faith involves a heart surrender to Jesus Christ. Every lost sinner in the world is lost because he says in his heart, "We will not have this man to reign over us" (Luke 19:14).

"And this is the condemnation, that light is come into the world, and men loved darkness rather than light, because their deeds were evil. For everyone that doeth evil hateth the light, neither cometh to the light, lest his deeds should be reproved. But he that doeth truth cometh to the light, that his deeds may be made manifest, that they are wrought in God" (John 3:19-21).

All sin, I say again, can be traced to rebellion against

authority, the authority of parents, the teacher, the husband, the boss, the government, and the authority of the Bible and God.

Obedience to Proper Authority—the Greatest Element in Character, in Righteousness and Godliness

All sin has its roots in rebellion. Hence, obedience to proper authority is the greatest element in personal righteousness. If citizens obey the laws there is no crime. If parents assume proper authority and children obey them, all problems between parent and children can be settled easily. If husbands take the high and holy responsibility given them by the Bible as heads of the wives and of the homes and if wives submit themselves to their own husbands ("Wives, submit yourselves unto your own husbands, as unto the Lord. For the husband is the head of the wife, even as Christ is the head of the church; and he is the saviour of the body. Therefore as the church is subject unto Christ, so let the wives be to their own husbands in every thing."—Eph. 5:22-24), then there will be no more divorce, no more faded love, no more broken homes. If servants obey their masters ("Servants, be obedient to them that are your masters according to the flesh, with fear and trembling, in singleness of your heart, as unto Christ"—Eph. 6:5) and masters and boss foremen exercise properly their God-given authority, the strikes, lockouts, sabotage, and industrial bloodshed will be gone forever. Obedience to proper authority is the most essential element in character. How important that children be taught obedience.

The baby bird is grown and out of the nest in a few weeks; kittens and dogs are grown in a few months; a calf is about grown in two years; a colt in from three to four years. Yet the child is not grown for eighteen or twenty years, not legally an adult, old enough to vote, until eighteen. A baby colt or calf can stand and run before it is a day old, while human babies cannot walk until nearly a year old, cannot talk intelligently for several years and do not even start school until about six years of age! It takes weeks to make a bird, twenty years to make a man or woman.

Why does the child mature so slowly compared to animals? Why does God leave a child under the protection of father and mother, dependent on them for support and care and teaching for twenty years? Without any possible doubt the child needs discipline, correction, training, long years of it, before he can be fit for adult life according to God's plan. To ignore God's plan that each child should have a long and careful, tender yet vigorous training is a wicked sin on the part of parents and often spells ruin to the child.

Parents Responsible for the Way Children Turn Out

God holds parents responsible for their children, responsible for them now and responsible for them hereafter. And the great men and women who are cited by the Bible as successful parents accept this responsibility.

Joshua called for the elders, and judges, the heads of tribes and families of Israel and said to them, "And if it seem evil unto you to serve the Lord, choose you this day whom ye will serve. . . but as for me and my house we will serve the Lord" (Josh. 24:15). This saintly old man assumed the responsibility for his entire household, for his wife, his children and his servants. "And Israel served the Lord all the days of Joshua, and all the days of the elders that overlived Joshua, and which had known all the works of the Lord, that he had done for Israel" (Josh. 24:31). That is a clear case of a father taking the responsibility of the entire family.

Abraham, the friend of God, also took the responsibility for his children. The Lord God revealed to Abraham all His plan concerning the destruction of Sodom and gave to him great and blessed promises, because, God said, "For I know him, that he will command his children and his household after him, and they shall keep the way of the Lord, to do justice and judgment; that the Lord may bring upon Abraham that which he hath spoken of him" (Gen. 18:19).

The beautiful life of Isaac may be traced largely to the commands and strict discipline of Abraham, no doubt.

In fact, the Bible plainly teaches that if a child is properly trained he will never depart from the right way, not even when he is old. "Train up a child in the way he should go; and when he is old, he will not depart from it" (Prov. 22:6).

Some parents rely on this Scripture and yet tell me, "Well, I know my boy has gone far in sin and has broken my heart in a wicked life, but some day, the Bible says, he will come back to his training and serve God." But that is not what the Bible says. The Scripture does *not* say that the child will depart from his training and turn to a life of sin, and later return. Instead, the Lord emphatically promises that when children are trained up in the way they should go *they will never depart from it,* not even when they are old!

You can clearly see that God holds the parents accountable for their children. The father and mother are accountable for the way the child lives, not only while he is at home but through the rest of his life.

God's Curse on Eli for Not Controlling His Sons

How strictly God holds parents to account for their children is illustrated in the case of Eli. Eli was the chief priest. His two sons, Hophni and Phinehas, were priests under him, and wicked men they were, violating the command of God about the sacrifices and committing terrible sin with the women who came to sacrifice. Eli remonstrated with them but did not enforce his command, neither were they disciplined nor taken from the priesthood. God sent a message by little Samuel. God charged Eli with this sin: "Thou honourest thy sons above me" (I Sam.

2:29). God had intended that Eli's house should walk before him in the priesthood forever but now the family was all rejected.

God said, "For I have told him that I will judge his house for ever for the iniquity which he knoweth; *because his sons made themselves vile, and he restrained them not.* And therefore I have sworn unto the house of Eli, that the iniquity of Eli's house shall not be purged with sacrifice nor offering for ever" (I Sam. 3:13,14).

Eli had not disciplined his sons when they were children and now that they were grown he did not restrain them. He remonstrated weakly but did not enforce his commands with the authority that was his. In God's sight that was a horrible sin. God held Eli, the father, accountable for all the sins of his sons. And the following chapter tells how the two sons were killed in God's anger, and Eli died also. The nation Israel was defeated in battle with the Philistines and the ark of God was taken captive. There the Scriptures take particular pains to declare all this evil came because God's man did not discipline his sons and did not make them do right. So parents are held accountable to God for so rearing their children that they will live godly lives.

Bible Warnings and Promises Concerning Whipping Children

I well know that many modern psychologists and educators argue against any strict enforcement of parental commands. They give many warnings against punishing children, fearing, they say, that one "may break the child's will." But I tell you frankly, after experience with my own six blessed youngsters, and after years of observation, that it is not as easy to break the child's will as you may have thought. There is considerably more danger that the child will break the parent's will! Children have plenty of will-power—yes, and even more "won't power."

Should children be whipped to make them mind, and

punished bodily for disobedience? If you should investigate scientifically, you would certainly find that children who were made to mind, children who were taught strict obedience by godly parents following the Bible command, turn out well.

But since your observation may be limited, let us go directly to the Bible. The Bible is the inspired Word of God. It is just as authoritative on how to raise children as it is on how to be saved. For a Christian the Bible is the inspired and infallible Word of God and must be the court of last resort. Then let us see what the Bible says about punishing children.

In chapter 1, we discussed several Scriptures in Proverbs. But let me mention two or three others here.

"Foolishness is bound in the heart of a child; but the rod of correction shall drive it far from him" (Prov. 22:15).

Children are precious and lovely. It is true as Wordsworth said,

> *"Not in utter nakedness, not in entire forgetfulness, but trailing clouds of glory do we come from God who is our home."*

He meant that children bring from Heaven a bit of glory and purity. How sweet they are! But we must not forget that "foolishness is bound in the heart of a child." The Bible says "they go astray as soon as they be born, speaking lies" (Ps. 58:3). David said about himself, and we might all say it truly, "Behold, I was shapen in iniquity; and in sin did my mother conceive me" (Ps. 51:5). The little child is kept safe by God's mercy until he reaches the time of accountability, but we must never forget the inborn taint of sin in the heart of every child. God says that "foolishness is bound in the heart of a child," and God gives that as the reason why children must be punished—to teach them not to sin. "The rod of correction shall drive it far from him."

If you do not want your child to be turned over to the natural wickedness of his heart, then you must drive it from him with the rod as well as by prayer and tears and godly example, and precepts, line upon line! Correction and discipline cannot change the heart of a child and make him a Christian, but they can teach him to hate sin and shame so that he will sincerely turn to Christ for forgiveness and salvation.

You may tell an arrogant youth that he must so reap what he sows, that "the wages of sin is death" (Rom. 6:23), that "the way of a transgressor is hard" (Prov. 13:15), but he will not believe it unless it was proven in his home. Every father is a type of God to his children. If the father does not punish him, why should the child believe that God will? If he has always gotten by without punishment, then Satan will find an easy dupe in such a child, reared where there was no law, no enforcement of right, no exercising of godly authority.

In Shamrock, Texas, there lived a family near me. The father was not a Christian, yet the strictness with which he reared his children was noticed by all. Some criticized and some approved. A grown son was expected to answer instantly, to obey cheerfully, and he did so! A beautiful grown daughter was never permitted to keep company with a young man whose morals were not right and every child had to be home by an appointed time each night. These rules were enforced by strict discipline.

There were two remarkable results. One was the love and reverence of this household for the father, which was beautiful to see. And the other result was this: although they had not been under Christian environment, I found the children remarkably approachable and easy to win to Christ. I found they had a sharp conscience for sin, a regard of law and order and authority. They were sensitive to the plain teachings of the Bible for sin and punishment and the need for a Saviour. And what a contrast these children were to other young people in the community, some of whom had Christian parents but had not been reared to respect authority and offer willing obedience! All the children, as

I recall, were soon won to Christ and had lovable and admirable Christian characters.

Whipping children will not only keep them from the penitentiary and keep them from a life of crime, but it will also keep them from Hell. That is what the verse above says. In countless cases, no doubt, there are people in Hell who could have been won to Christ. They could have been convicted of sin and brought to fear of judgment and heartfelt repentance, had they been taught that sin is a wicked, hellish rebellion against the authority of God, and that sin must inevitably bring grief and sorrow and shame and punishment! This is not the word of men but the Word of God. The inspired Word of God says, "Thou shalt beat him with the rod and deliver his soul from hell."

"The rod and reproof give wisdom; but a child left to himself bringeth his mother to shame" (Prov. 29:15).

Here again we see part of the character-molding effect of correction and discipline. The Bible says that "the fear of the Lord is the beginning of wisdom" (Prov. 1:7). The proper reverential fear of father and mother in authority is easily transferred to an attitude of reverence of godly fear toward God. In other words, the punishment of sin gives a right understanding of what sin is and what its results must be. By punishment children learn what is justice and righteousness. They learn self-control and the restraint of a developed conscience and they learn to respect the rights of others. How easy it is to see that the Bible is true and that "the rod and reproof give wisdom," and likewise every one of us have seen that a "child left to himself bringeth his mother to shame." The mother has been given long years in which to develop true wisdom in the child, by strict enforcement of the law of right and wrong, and by careful instruction that sin can not pay, but that right always brings blessed rewards. The father who told me his boy was in the penitentiary, but would not believe what God said in Proverbs 22:6, did not do that. How many brokenhearted mothers would have been spared the shame brought them by a prodigal child if they had simply used the rod and reproof to give wisdom!

"Correct thy son and he shall give thee rest; yea, he shall give delight unto thy soul" (Prov. 29:17).

Punishment brings rest! We would think not. We would think that punishment would bring more rebellious unrest of mind. But when punishment is administered lovingly, and under the blessings of God, and thoroughly enough to get results, the punishment brings rest. With the hardened criminal in the penitentiary, still a rebel against society and against God this may not be true, but with a tenderhearted child in the home, God says it is true. The child will get rest and therefore will give rest to the parents and their souls will be delighted.

I remember with a sharp sense of comedy how in my childhood, if any of us had a licking coming we were consumed with dread and perhaps resentment until it was done. But afterwards, we were back in the fellowship of the home. How good it was to have the punishment over and how sweet the peace!

And I remember how astonished I was, as a young father, when I learned that sometimes the quickest way to get a nervous, irritable child to sleep was to give her a sound spanking! Yet I had thought to spank a child would make her most upset and so nervous that she could not sleep. On the contrary, when a spanking stops the rebellion inside, the nerve tension is released, and the child submits peaceably to the will of the father and mother and lies still and restfully sleeps! So many, many times the only way to have rest for the parent is to get matters settled with a convincing correction.

Father, your child will some day be away from home and out from under your care, and then will you be haunted with fear and anguish? Will you be uneasy lest he submit to the lure of wine and women and song? Or will you have sweet rest in heart, knowing that self-control and strong character and obedience were settled by careful teaching and prayerful, vigorous discipline whenever necessary in days gone by? How sweet is the rest in the heart, the delight in the soul, that is promised the parent who corrects the child as commanded by the Lord and then trusts God to bring His promises to pass!

I have brought you the Word of God. Those who are not willing to take God's Word on this matter, as on every other matter, should never call themselves Christians.

I well know that parents have need of the wisdom of Solomon in rearing children. These commands of God do not mean that whipping children is the only duty of parents toward them. Ephesians 6:4 says, "Ye fathers, provoke not your children to wrath, but bring them up in the nurture and admonition of the Lord." Children need more than admonition—they need nurture also. Children need love, counsel; they need godly examples before them every day. Yet the importance which the Bible gives to this doctrine of the correction and discipline of children cannot be safely ignored. It might well be the single most important factor in rearing children into godly men and women, well adjusted, good citizens, dutiful husbands and wives. In some cases, certainly, the lack of discipline makes it impossible to win children to Christ, since they have no conception of sin, no love of right, no fear of punishment.

How quickly the crime situation could be cleared up if children were taught obedience and respect for authority at home! And wives would not be rebellious, self-seeking and unfaithful, in most cases, surely, if they had been taught obedient submission to authority and adjustment to the rights of others in childhood.

No man is fit to be President who has not been a law-abiding citizen. No man is ready to give orders until he has learned to obey orders. Consider the rigorous discipline of West Point

Academy where U.S. army officers are trained. So doubtless no man is fit to be husband and father who has not learned obedience to law and order in the home. Divorces have increased along with desertion and other family troubles, just as fast as homes have broken down in the discipline of children.

The most important institution in the world is not the government, not the school, not even the church, but the home. And the most important element for children in the home is not the physical care of children, providing food and clothing and shelter, but the discipline and growth of children.

I beg every parent who reads this to prayerfully consider your duty in the light of God's Word. Why not husband and wife together check up on your failure? Why not a regular plan of daily worship and include Bible study and prayer? Why not definitely prune out of your lives that which would be a bad example before your children? Why not make a new dedication of your whole lives to God as parents?

And then, believing God's Word and loving your children, why not set out to please God and safeguard your children's future by vigorous discipline, whenever needed, coupled with much prayer and love! God's way works. I beg parents to try it and see.

Mrs. Wesley's Godly Way of Rearing Children. . .

How were John Wesley and Charles Wesley, leaders in the great evangelical movement in England, founders of Methodism, reared? By what manner were such godly men, so well-controlled, so wholly given to the Lord, so brilliant in mind, so tender in conscience, so unswerving in principle, developed? Their mother, Susannah Wesley, taught them to fear the rod when they were a year old. So she herself says, and John Wesley himself published her statement.

The holy lives of these saintly men, John and Charles Wesley, grew out of the godly discipline of the home. That the Wesleys themselves believed, and the Scriptures bear them out. Susannah Wesley believed the Scripture, "The rod and reproof bring wisdom; but a child left to himself bringeth his mother to shame" (Prov. 29:15). She believed the Scripture, "The blueness of a wound cleanseth away evil; so do stripes the inward parts of the belly" (Prov. 20:30).

She believed the teaching of the Scriptures that one who is not chastised is treated as a bastard, not as a legitimate son (Heb. 12:7,8).

In *The Heart of John Wesley's Journal* is published a letter from Mrs. Wesley to her son, part of which we give here:

July 24, 1732

"Dear Son:

"According to your desire, I have collected the principal rules I observed in educating my family; which I now send you as they occurred to my mind (if you think they can be of use to any) dispose of them in what order you please.

"When turned a year old (and some before), they were taught to fear the rod, and to cry softly; by which means they escaped abundance of correction they might otherwise have had; and that most odious noise of the crying of children was rarely heard in the house but the family usually lived in as much quietness as if there had not been a child among them.

"In order to form the minds of children, the first thing to be done is to conquer their will and bring them to an obedient temper. To inform the understanding is a work of time, and must with children proceed by slow degrees as they are able to bear it: but the subjecting the will is a thing which must be done at once; and the sooner the better. For by neglecting timely correction, they will contract a stubbornness and obstinacy which is hardly ever after conquered; and never, without using such severity as would be as painful to me as to the child.

"In the esteem of the world they pass for kind and indulgent, whom I call cruel, parents, who permit their children to get habits which they know must be afterwards broken. Nay, some are so stupidly fond, as in sport to teach their children to do things which, in a while after, they have severely beaten them for doing.

"Whenever a child is corrected, it must be conquered; and this will be no hard matter to do, if it be not grown headstrong by too much indulgence. And when the will of a child is totally subdued, and it is brought to revere and stand in awe of the parents, then a great many childish follies and inadvertences may be passed by.

"Some should be overlooked and taken no notice of, and others mildly reproved; but no willful transgression ought ever to be forgiven children, without chastisement, less or more, as the nature and circumstances of the offense require.

"I insist upon conquering the will of children betimes, because this is the only strong and rational foundation of a religious education; without which both precept and example will be ineffectual. But when this is thoroughly done, then a child is capable of being governed by the reason and piety of its parents, till its own understanding comes to maturity, and the principles of religion have taken root in the mind.

"I cannot yet dismiss this subject. As self-will is the root of all sin and misery, so whatever cherishes this in children insures their after-wretchedness and irreligion; whatever checks and mortifies it promotes their future happiness and piety. This is still more evident if we further consider that religion is nothing else than the doing of the will of God, and not our own; that the one grand impediment to our temporal and eternal happiness being this self-will, no indulgences of it can be trivial, no denial unprofitable. Heaven or Hell depends on this. So that the parent who studies to subdue it in his child works together with God in the renewing and saving a soul. The parent who indulges it does the Devil's work, makes religion impracticable, salvation unattainable; and does all that in him lies to damn his child, soul and body, forever.

They Had Nothing They Cried for

"The children of this family were taught, as soon as they could speak, the Lord's prayer, which they were made to say at rising and bedtime constantly; to which as they grew bigger, were added a short prayer for their parents, and some collects; a short catechism, and some portion of Scripture, as their memories could bear.

"They were very early made to distinguish the Sabbath from other days; before they could well speak or go. They were as soon taught to be still at family prayers; and to ask a blessing immediately after, which they used to do by signs before they could kneel or speak.

"They were quickly made to understand they might have nothing they cried for, and instructed to speak handsomely for what they wanted. They were not suffered to ask even the lowest servant for ought without saying, 'Pray give me such a thing'; and the servant was chided, if she ever let them omit that word."

Thus Susannah Wesley, saint of God, reared those great men whose influence kept millions out of Hell. Surely she proved well enough the truth of the Scripture that though "A child left to himself bringeth his mother to shame" the converse is also true, "The rod and reproof give wisdom," and "Correct thy son, and he shall give delight unto thy soul."

Summary of Mrs. Wesley's Child-Rearing

1. Eating between meals not allowed.
2. As children they are to be in bed by eight p.m.
3. They are required to take medicine without complaining.
4. Subdue self-will in a child, and thus work together with God to save a child's soul.
5. Teach a child to pray as soon as he can speak.
6. Require all to be still during Family Worship.
7. Give them nothing that they cry for, and only that which they ask for politely.
8. To prevent lying, punish no fault which is first confessed and repented of.
9. Never allow a sinful act to go unpunished.
10. Never punish a child twice for a single offense.
11. Commend and reward good behavior.
12. Any attempt to please, even if poorly performed, should be commended.
13. Preserve property rights, even in smallest matters.
14. Strictly observe all promises.
15. Require no daughter to work before she can read well.
16. Teach children to fear the rod.

Start a Family Altar Today

Set a Time Daily When the Whole Family Reads Together at Least a Chapter of Bible, Has Circle of Prayer, Learns Verses

Stop Raising Hippies! Help Save America! You Can Guarantee All Your Children Will Be Godly, Christian Citizens Serving Christ

"And these words, which I command thee this day, shall be in thine heart: And thou shalt teach them diligently unto thy children, and shalt talk of them when thou sittest in thine house, and when thou walkest by the way, and when thou liest down, and when thou risest up. And thou shalt bind them for a sign upon thine hand, and they shall be as frontlets between thine eyes. And thou shalt write them upon the posts of thy house, and on thy gates."—Deut. 6:6-9.

By testing congregations all over America I have come to the conclusion that less than one out of ten fundamental Christian families regularly have a time of daily Bible reading and prayer together. And surprisingly, probably not more than one out of three or four fundamental Bible-believing preachers has such a daily family altar of Bible reading and prayer. That is so shocking that we feel we should urge pastors everywhere to help us, and we should set out to get 10,000 more families having a daily time of such devotions together.

How explicit, how positive, is the scriptural command above about having in the heart the Word of God and teaching it diligently to the children; when sitting, walking, lying down, rising up, carrying Scriptures on the body, writing them on the posts of the house and on the gates!

In the preceding chapter Moses had just recounted again the Ten Commandments which were first given in Exodus, chapter 20. At Mount Sinai the people had said to Moses:

"Go thou near, and hear all that the Lord our God shall say: and speak thou unto us all that the Lord our God shall speak unto thee; and we will hear it, and do it. And the Lord heard the voice of your words, when ye spake unto me; and the Lord said unto me, I have heard the voice of the words of this people, which they have spoken unto thee: they have well said all that they have spoken. O that there were such an heart in them, that they would fear me, and keep all my commandments always, that it might be well with them, and with their children for ever!"— Deut. 5:27-29.

Here is a promise that God made again and again to Israel, if they would have a heart to fear Him and keep all His commandments, "that it might be well with them, and with their children for ever."

That promise is as pertinent to us as to Israel. For in Galatians 3:9 Paul is inspired to say, "So then they which be of faith are blessed with faithful Abraham," and verse 29 says it even stronger, "And if ye be Christ's, then are ye Abraham's seed, and heirs according to the promise."

First Corinthians 10:11 tells us about the things that happened to Israel: "Now all these things happened unto them for ensamples: and they are written for our admonition, upon whom the ends of the world are come." It is true that the Old Testament contained not only the moral law but the ceremonial law (the

Jewish Sabbath in this case), and the ceremonial laws are fulfilled and are not required of us. But God's eternal principle is the same. Those who teach diligently His precious Word have a right to these promises. It is a way to guarantee that you have godly children, good citizens. The way to a real Christian home must include, as a major factor, teaching diligently the Word of God to the children and enforcing its commands.

What a shame that all over America we find hippies, rebels, school drop-outs, dopeheads, and youngsters from nominal Christian homes. We find sex immorality, the draft card burners, defilers of the flag, enemies of the police and of the government, hating their fathers and mothers from the same kind of homes. You who do not have a family altar and the definite impact of the Bible on your home life are raising these hippies, which means the destruction of America, unless the trend is reversed. Oh, ten thousand Christian homes reading the Bible, loving it, being taught it diligently, memorizing much of it, with godly discipline, would mean that Christian families in America would be rearing presidents, senators, governors, university presidents and professors and preachers of great churches. If America is to be saved it must be by Christian homes where God can mold the lives of the people through the Word of God and Christian discipline and teaching.

I. THE BIBLE IN THE HOME THE ONLY HOPE OF OUR CIVILIZATION

Christian morality comes only from the historic Christian faith, the old-time religion. It comes from knowing and loving the Word of God.

More than a century ago religious convictions and influence had so declined in England that the country seemed about to follow the convulsions of the French Revolution. The Gospel was rarely preached in the state churches—the Anglican church. The clergy themselves were usually Deists, unconverted, unbelievers in the historic Christian faith and given to gambling and drunkenness and bribery. The government was corrupt on nearly all levels. Laborers were exploited. Little children were sometimes compelled to work twelve hours a day in the mines and elsewhere. Prisons were disgraceful. There were almost no hospitals, no homes for orphans and very little public education. Unrest and wickedness seethed everywhere.

And then John Wesley and his helpers were used of God to bring about a great revival. He preached to thousands in the fields. He was stoned, slandered, abused, shut out of the churches, yet thousands were saved, and a conscience of England revived. Those influenced by the Wesleyan revival helped lead in abolishing slavery and making decent laws in caring for the orphans and for the sick.

1. Why Democracy Fails When Christian Morality Fails

There can be no Bible morality without honest Bible preaching and teaching. The principle of democracy is a greatly loved principle, but there is one fatal flaw in democratic majority rule. When the majority of people get corrupt, then they pass laws to get what they can get without principle.

There are more poor people than rich people, so they pass laws to take away the wealth from those who have earned it and give it to those who didn't earn it. When the majority goes wrong, then there are more people who drink liquor than those who do not, so they abolish prohibition laws. Then when the majority is corrupt, and they repeal the laws against pornographic literature, divorce is made easy, and the majority begins to press for the right to murder unborn babies (abortion). When the majority is corrupt, then they vote that everybody must have free medicare, free social security, minimum wage, full pay for a four-day week, etc.

When the people are corrupt, then instead of seeking to get

their just dues, the labor unions seek to get all the money they can, for less work all the time. When people do not have holy convictions abour morality, then they continually vote to spend more money, get the government further in debt, owing millions that can never be paid.

So, as in Greece and Rome and France and many other countries, a democracy without the morality of the Christian religion becomes corrupt, lawlessness becomes rampant, people's lives and property are not safe, and eventually some dictator comes along who promises the people security and law enforcement and he gives it, though he takes away their liberties.

2. Delighting in the Scriptures, the Key to Prosperity

Loving and obeying the Scripture while avoiding evil men is the secret of perfect success for the individual, as we learn in Psalm 1:1-3:

"Blessed is the man that walketh not in the counsel of the ungodly, nor standeth in the way of sinners, nor sitteth in the seat of the scornful. But his delight is in the law of the Lord; and in his law doth he meditate day and night. And he shall be like a tree planted by the rivers of water, that bringeth forth his fruit in his season; his leaf also shall not wither; and whatsoever he doeth shall prosper."

What a wonderful promise! Prosperity in everything one lays his hand to, if he avoids evil company and meditates day and night in the Word of God!

The same precious truth was given Joshua:

"There shall not any man be able to stand before thee all the days of thy life: as I was with Moses, so I will be with thee: I will not fail thee, nor forsake thee. Be strong and of a good courage: for unto this people shalt thou divide for an inheritance the land, which I sware unto their fathers to give them. Only be thou

strong and very courageous, that thou mayest observe to do according to all the law, which Moses my servant commanded thee: turn not from it to the right hand or to the left, that thou mayest prosper whithersoever thou goest. This book of the law shall not depart out of thy mouth; but thou shalt meditate therein day and night, that thou mayest observe to do according to all that is written therein: for then thou shalt make thy way prosperous, and then thou shalt have good success."—Josh. 1:5-8.

But here in the Scriptures quoted in Deuteronomy we find that the same blessed promise holds good for nations and for peoples and families. The family that delights in the Word of God, loves it, teaches it to the children, meditates in it—that family will be prospered, the children will turn out to be moral, godly, good citizens, happy, successful Christians, the Scripture says. The Bible is the only hope for our civilization.

3. The Home Is the Only Place Where the Bible Can Be Taught as It Ought to Be

It is true that the people who regularly attend churches that have godly, well-taught, Spirit-filled preachers, learn a lot of Scripture from the preaching. But it is only fair to say that only a small proportion of Christians attend churches where there is regular teaching of the Word of God from the pulpit. At most, it would be only a text or a short passage of Scripture before the sermon. Those who do not study the Bible for themselves but depend only upon the preaching they hear are always woefully ignorant of the Word of God.

Good, sound Sunday schools do teach some of the Word of God. Actually, Sunday school lessons do not give more than a relatively few selected Scriptures for study in the year's time. Even in good fundamental churches where the teachers are well prepared, a thirty-minute Sunday school lesson once a week will never teach as much Bible as people need. The thirty minutes of

Christian emphasis in Sunday school once a week cannot hold its own in influence against many hours of teaching in the public schools, plus all the influence of the TV, the cheap literature that is available everywhere, and the influence of evil companions.

No, the one place where the Bible can be fully taught daily and adequately is in the home.

Millions of people feel, as I do, that the Warren Supreme Court, a left-wing court, in re-defining the laws of America, did great harm in limiting the matter of prayer and Bible reading in public schools. Separation of church and state, provided in our Constitution, did not mean that our founding fathers were against the Bible. They were simply against any state-controlled and compelled religion and insisted that there be chaplains to have prayer in Congress and in each branch of the armed services. Public officials are sworn in on the Bible, taking an oath before God. Our coins proclaim, "In God we trust." Both our national anthem, "Star Spangled Banner," and our national hymn, "America," call on the people to trust God to take care of America. It would be perfectly proper to have Bible reading and prayer voluntarily, without any denominational propaganda, in the public schools, according to our Constitution but not according to the Warren Court. I say, I think they were wrong.

However, the simple fact is that in most of America the churches could have released-time sessions for teaching the Word of God and they usually do not take advantage of the opportunity. And if the school had, let us say, fifteen minutes or thirty minutes a day for reading the Bible, there could not be detailed teaching on controversial points where there is great difference among Christians. Even if we had liberty, the Bible teaching in the school will not fill the need.

But what hypocrisy it is for Christian people to indignantly blame the action of the Supreme Court about no Bible reading and no prayer in the schools when they do not have it at home!

There is no law to prevent you from praying with your children. There is no law to prevent you from reading the Bible in your home and teaching your children the Bible. And it is a poor kind of escapism to blame the courts for forbidding Bible teaching in the schools, when you do not sincerely care enough about it to have it in your own home.

The only place we can adequately teach our children the Bible, as it ought to be taught, is in the home. Let's have all the help we can from the Sunday school, the preaching, Daily Vacation Bible School, Child Evangelism and summer camps. It still remains that those who attend only these outside agencies will have only a smattering of Bible knowledge, and they will not have the wholehearted devotion to the Bible, when it is not valued at home and read and taught with holy zeal.

II. BUT IT IS THE COMMANDMENTS GOD EMPHASIZES HERE

Read again that passage in Deuteronomy 6:6-9. "These words, which I command thee this day" are those that should be in our hearts and those we should diligently teach our children. And the Scripture has just gone over the Ten Commandments and related commands. It is true that the principle of this Scripture applies to the whole Bible as we have it, not only to the part of the law that Israel then had. But here is a basic summary of all human duty as given in the Ten Commandments.

The first four commands, including the ceremonial command of the Sabbath which was applied to the Jews, refer to man's duty to God. We are not to make images, we are not to make idols, we are not to bow down to them or serve them, we are not to take God's name in vain. The last six commandments sum up our duty to all mankind. We are to honor fathers and mothers, we are not to murder, not to commit adultery, not to lie, not to steal, not to covet. Rightly interpreted, as they were interpreted in the New Tesament, they involve all morality and righteousness. Jesus summed them up as being some detailed expressions of the great commandment, that one should love God with all his heart, mind, soul and strength and love his neighbor as himself.

1. Then the First Basic Truths of the Bible Are for Morality and Righteousness

There is a good reason why God gave the law of the Old Testament before He gave the New Testament. Men are to know they are sinners before they feel the need for a Saviour. Though repentance and faith are the two faces of that heart decision that God requires to make one a child of God, repentance is always mentioned first when they are mentioned together. You face the matter of sin before you face the matter of forgiveness and salvation. The home that establishes a family altar, then, must set out to stress the *commandments* of God, what a righteous and holy God requires.

2. That Means That in the Home, Parents Must Emphasize the "Thou Shalt Nots"

There is a foolish teaching abroad based on the Dewey philosophy of education, a philosophy of Satan, that you should never say "no" to a child, that you should never say "you must not." People foolishly say that if you didn't make it against the law to take dope, many young people wouldn't take it. They say that with a law against drinking liquor, more people would drink it. That simply is not so. It is true there is a tendency for rebellion against God and against the law and against right, against authority, inherent in the carnal human nature. Christian parents dare not cotton to that wicked nature. The Bible says, "Thou shalt not. . .," and the foolish education professors are not as wise as God. God said to Adam and Eve in the Garden of Eden, "Thou shalt not eat of the tree of the knowledge of good and evil." In the Ten Commandments God says, "Thou shalt not," about idolatry, about profanity, about murder and adultery and lying and stealing and covetousness and rebellion against authority in the home. The Bible philosophy must prevail in the home which has a family altar.

3. It Necessarily Follows That God's Authority in the Home Rests in the Parents and They Must Enforce His Rules

The command, "Thou shalt teach them diligently unto thy children," means that parents speak with certain authority. Pupils must respect teachers. Sons and daughters must respect fathers and mothers, and listen to them. Parental authority is involved in this family altar business.

Read again the commands about whipping children in Proverbs 13:24; Proverbs 19:18; Proverbs 20:30; Proverbs 22:15; Proverbs 23:13,14; Proverbs 29:15,17 and in Ephesians 6:4 where fathers are commanded to "bring them up in the nurture and admonition of the Lord." The word "nurture" in the original really means "discipline" or "enforced discipline." The Greek word used here is the one used for chastisement in several New Testament Scriptures. And in the same Mosaic law, Deuteronomy 21:18-21 provides that with a rebellious son who cannot be controlled the father and mother have a right to bring the matter to the elders of the city and demand that he be stoned to death.

Just as in Psalm 1:1-3 the blessings promised for those who meditate day and night in the Word of God are conditioned on their turning from evil companions, so here it is only fair to say that the blessings promised to those who teach their children the Bible are conditioned on the godly authority of the parents.

In this matter, of course, God intended the man, the husband or father, to be the ruler in the home. The wife is to be subject to her husband, as we learn in Genesis 3:16; Ephesians 5:22-24; I Peter 3:1,2. Joshua, the head of the home, said, "As for me and my house, we will serve the Lord" (Josh. 24:15). God even provided that a man should teach his wife the Scriptures and answer her Bible questions. "Let your women keep silence in the churches: for it is not permitted unto them to speak; but they are commanded to be under obedience, as also saith the law. And if they will learn any thing, let them ask their husbands at home: for it is a shame for women to speak in the church" (I Cor. 14:34,35).

There can be no godliness without authority. The authority of God, the authority of the Bible, the authority of parents, and the authority of government all stand or fall together.

III. "TEACH THEM DILIGENTLY"

So says the Word of God. These are strong words.

1. Give the Word of God Daily Priority in the Home

One who takes seriously the instruction in Deuteronomy 6:6-9 must be impressed that the Bible is not simply one item of many, is not a minor matter and not only a major one, but it is a controlling factor of the whole life of a home.

First of all, the Word of God, the commands of God, "shall be in thine heart." The commands of God should be memorized, not only in the mind but in the heart, the seat of affections. A devoted love of the Bible so that one memorizes much of it, is here commanded.

And then this Word of God shall be taught diligently to the children. Parents shall talk of the Scriptures "when thou sittest in thine house, and when thou walkest by the way, and when thou liest down, and when thou risest up." That means every problem that comes up in the home will be dealt with in the light of the Scriptures. That means even with the children that the commands, God's Word, the promises, the warnings must be applied day and night. And the Scriptures shall be bound on the parents' hands and as frontlets between the eyes. Even if that be a figure of speech, it means surely that parents shall keep visible somewhere a constant reminder of God's law and the commands of God. They shall be written upon the posts of the house and upon the gates.

Dr. G. Campbell Morgan tells us that when he married, he was very proud of his little home until his father came to see him. Proudly the young husband showed his father through the home, waiting for this comment. Did he like it?

The father simply said that one could not tell whether it was a home of a Christian or an infidel. Not a motto on the wall, not a Scripture verse, nothing clearly reminding one that this was a house of a man of God. Morgan saw the point and so placed mottoes and Scriptures on the wall of every room.

2. Christian Homes, Then, Should See That the Bible Is Read Not Only by Individual Members but Publicly as a Group to Learn, Memorize, to Comment

Then if we take to heart God's commands about the home, parents must supervise their children in memorizing portions of Scripture. Into the plastic minds and hearts of little children, parents must engrave, never to be forgotten, the Word of God. Children should learn, of course, the Ten Commandments, the Lord's Prayer, the Beatitudes; they should learn a collection of Scriptures on the plan of salvation, on the security of a believer, on prayer and its answers, on Christian love and fellowship, on praises to God, on dependence for daily needs and fellowship, on forgiveness and love and soul winning. Surely the family as a whole ought to memorize many whole chapters.

In our home all of us memorized Psalms 1,8,15,19, 23,24,34,37,100,121,126,127. We memorized Matthew 28, the resurrection story, and said it from memory every Easter Sunday morning at the breakfast table. We memorized Luke, chapter 2, the story of the birth of Jesus. We memorized John, chapters 1,3, and 14; I Corinthians 13; Romans 8 and 12; Philippians 4. We memorized literally thousands of verses of Scripture.

That means that some of this work was done at the time of family devotions when we read the Bible, then it was followed up in individual devotions and study, and then when we came together either at the regular family devotions or casually at any time while we were together, we repeated for each other the Scriptures we had learned.

To teach the Scriptures "diligently" means to memorize, to drill, to enforce the Scriptures.

3. How to Have a Family Altar?

Any serious effort to teach children the Bible and to be good Christians means a regular scheduled time, part of the family program every day.

What time is best? In our own home, Mrs. Rice and I found that the evening is not the best time. I was often engaged in preaching services. It was not convenient to keep little children awake late or to wake them up for devotions. Besides, it is far better to start the day with Scripture and prayer with the whole family.

We tried it before breakfast, but that interfered somewhat with the meal. Warm foods got cold, and the toast burned. We soon found that immediately after breakfast was for us the best time in the day. Everybody was required to be at breakfast. Everybody must take part in the Bible reading and prayer. As soon as they could manage to read haltingly, little children were allowed to read one verse when it came their turn.

The importance the Bible gives to teaching children the Word of God and His commands means that this time must be religiously kept, it must have an absolute priority over other more ordinary matters. When in our home one of our six girls sometimes said with dismay, "But, Daddy, we will be late for school!" I simply said that we had to have family devotions even if they were late for school, and warned that the next time they must get up in time. We had family devotions whether every girl had her hair combed, whether beds were made or lesson prepared.

Families simply will not keep up family devotions if other things are allowed to postpone it or if it is not made a part of the daily unvarying schedule. Character is not made up of holy vows and aspirations. It is made up of habits following those vows. One is not just a good Christian because he loves the Bible and intends to study it. One becomes a good Christian when the Bible becomes so much a part of his daily schedule that he feels he must not miss it and would be miserable if he did.

The Bible must have priority. Have family devotions even if you have company. Have family devotions on holidays, on Sundays. Have family devotions if some member is sick. Have family devotions if the alarm clock fails and you are running behind time. Only if the Bible is given a priority will it have the all-compelling effect of godliness and happiness in the home which God planned for it.

How should Bible reading be done? Sometimes the father reads the Bible aloud to others. That is good, but we think that not the best way. Young minds wander. A child might sit quietly but his thinking be miles away. So we found it best to read in succession around the table. We would read one chapter or if it were Psalms, perhaps two or more, each day. I would read the first two verses, then clockwise around the table every child would read two verses and back to me again; around and around until we finished the chapter. Thus everybody had to keep the place in mind to know when his turn came to read.

Occasionally Father or Mother should call attention to some verse that is especially good and suggest that a bracket be put about that verse, and memorize it and you should return to it the next day for review. Occasionally there ought to be brief discussion. "Grace, what do you think verse 13 means?" Or after the reading, "Elizabeth, what verse do you like best in this chapter?"

I suggest that the reading be in the King James Version of the Bible. So-called "modern language" versions are usually paraphrases and not very accurate and sometimes with liberal, inaccurate rendering. The King James Version is the Bible of the people. It has the most beautiful language. The idea that the language of the King James Version of the Bible is archaic, hard to understand, is rather silly. I taught Shakespeare to college freshmen and sophomores, and the language of Shakespeare is ten times more archaic and obsolete than is the King James Bible.

Enjoy the Bible. If Dad and Mother find it sweet and blessed and if the family regularly prays for God to be with them in their devotions, they will find it the happiest time of the day. Visitors who come to our home have again and again remarked years later that the happiest memory of their visit was the family devotions.

And then we would pray in a circle around the table. I would begin the prayer, then each one would follow in his own way, asking God for His blessing, asking help for the chores and duties of the day, asking for healing for someone who was sick, asking for help to win some particular soul, asking for help in the school work. Tiny children who cannot read the Bible can be taught a little memorized prayer so they can have part and soon they can pray from the heart.

And the family altar is a time also to praise good deeds, to rebuke quarrels, to settle problems. And besides, it means there is such close contact between parents and children that any time during the day (and sometimes during the night) a child will feel free to come to Dad or Mother for more prayer, or for help about a burden, or to confess a sin. There is no "generation gap" in the family where the authority of Father and Mother is clearly recognized and enforced, and where they have family devotions together.

How long will devotions take? Often not more than fifteen or twenty minutes; but what a precious time together!

In Jesus' Name, Start Today!

In every home where someone reads this, if you do not have a regular scheduled time of family devotions, Bible reading and prayer together, I beg you, begin today.

I suggest as follows:

1. That husband and wife talk it over and fully agree and select a time when the whole family can be together. Talk it over with the whole family. No child can veto it, but children might feel free to suggest any problem about the time. And then when it is settled, it is to become a settled matter, as unchanging as the law of the Medes and Persians! Everybody gets up in time or everybody leaves whatever other occupations in which they may be employed.

2. Start with reading one chapter. Perhaps you should start first to read through the book of Matthew. Read through the twenty-eight chapters on twenty-eight consecutive days. Or you may like to start in Genesis. Sometimes when one book is finished it may be well to skip to the Psalms or to another part of the New Testament for a refreshing change.

And then let us say frankly, the head of the family must simply stand up and require everybody to be present, everybody to take part. That kind of family devotions requires family authority in the home.

If you will set out to have family devotions regularly, I suggest that husband and wife decide and then as a committal fill out this form here and mail it to me. That will mean that you will feel you have committed yourself and that the matter is clear in your mind, and it will help me to know that you are setting out to have a really Christian home. I beg you to decide it and send me word today.

Evangelist John R. Rice, Editor
THE SWORD OF THE LORD
P. O. Box 1099
Murfreesboro, Tennessee 37130

Dear Brother Rice:

Today we have decided to definitely now commit ourselves that we will undertake to have a daily time of family devotions, reading the Bible, at least a chapter each day with the whole family and with a circle of prayer.

Time preferred ______________________________

Number of children in the family ______________________

With what book in the Bible are you beginning
the daily reading together? ____________________

Signed: Husband ____________________________

Wife ____________________________

Address ______________________________

____

(See next page)

How Blessed Is Our House

Arr. by Grace Rice MacMullen

Words and Music by
John R. Rice

How bles - sed is our house when God is there;
We read there the Bi - ble, To - ge - ther we pray,
Our fa - ther is God - ly, and hon - est and wise,
Dear mo - ther, so pat - ient, so lov - ing and kind,
With food in our lard - er, with joy in our hearts,

A place of con - tent - ment, a house of prayer.
We plead there for mer - cy, and help for each day.
We see we must do what is right in his eyes.
She feeds us and teach - es, she sees that we mind.
With love for our house - hold, for each one a part.

Where Je - sus the Sav - iour is trust - ed and known;
We find the Lord with us; We live in His care.
He prays with us, loves us, is Head of us all.
Her arms such a shel - ter, a - round us to cling.
With Christ as our Sav - iour, our God and our friend,

How bles - sed is our house, with God in our home!
En - joy His pro - vis - ion, His love dai - ly share.
He chast - ens, for - gives us, when - ev - er we fall.
Her home is her pal - ace, her hus - band a king.
How bles - sed our home is from now to the end.

Chorus
Our home........., Our home........., with love and with
prayer. How bles-sed is our house, For God is there!

Betsey and I Are Out

Draw up the papers, lawyer, and make 'em good and stout;
Things at home are crossways, and Betsey and I are out.
We, who have worked together so long as man and wife,
Must pull in single harness the rest of our nat'ral life.

"What is the matter?" say you. I swan it's hard to tell!
Most of the years behind us we've passed by very well;
I have no other woman, she has no other man—
Only we've lived together as long as we ever can.

So I have talked with Betsey, and Betsey has talked with me,
So we've agreed together that we can't never agree;
Not that we've catched each other in any terrible crime;
We've been a-gathering this for years, a little at a time.

There was a stock of temper we both had for a start,
Though we never suspected 'twould take us two apart;
I had my various failings, bred in the flesh and bone;
And Betsey, like all good women, had a temper of her own.

First thing I remember whereon we disagreed
Was something concerning Heaven—a difference in our creed;
We arg'ed the thing at breakfast, we arg'ed the thing at tea,
And the more we arg'ed the question the more we didn't agree.

And the next that I remember was when we lost a cow;
She had kicked the bucket for certain, the question was only—
  How?
I held my own opinion, and Betsey another had;
And when we were done a-talkin', we both of us was mad.

And the next that I remember, it started in a joke;
But full for a week it lasted, and neither of us spoke.
And the next was when I scolded because she broke a bowl;
And she said I was mean and stingy, and hadn't any soul.

And so that bowl kept pourin' dissensions in our cup;
And so that blamed old cow was always a-comin' up;
And so that Heaven we arg'ed no nearer to us got,
But it gave us a taste of somethin' a thousand times as hot.

And so the thing kept workin', and all the self-same way:
Always somethin' to arg'e, and somethin' sharp to say;
And down on us came the neighbors, a couple dozen strong,
And lent their kindest service for to help the thing along.

And there has been days together—and many a weary week—
We was both of us cross and crabbed, and both too proud
to speak;
And I have been thinkin' and thinkin', the whole of the winter
and fall,
If I can't live kind with a woman, why, then, I won't at all.

And so I have talked with Betsey, and Betsey has talked
with me,
And we have agreed together that we can't never agree;
And what is hers shall be hers, and what is mine shall be mine;
And I'll put it in the agreement, and take it to her to sign.

Write on the paper, lawyer—the very first paragraph—
Of all the farm and live-stock that she shall have her half;
For she has helped to earn it, through many a weary day:
And it's nothing more than justice that Betsey has her pay.

Give her the house and homestead: a man can thrive and roam,
But women are skeery critters, unless they have a home;
And I have always determined, and never failed to say,
That my wife never should want a home if I was taken away.

There is a little hard cash that's drawin' tol'rable pay:
Just a few thousand dollars laid by for a rainy day;
Safe in the hands of good men, and easy to get at;
Put in another clause there, and give her half of that.

Yes, I see you smile, Sir, at my givin' her so much;
Yes, divorces is cheap, Sir, but I take no stock in such!
True and fair I married her, when she was blithe and young;
And Betsey was al'ays good to me—exceptin' with her tongue.

Once, when I was young as you, and not so smart, perhaps,
For me she mittened a lawyer, and several other chaps;
And all of them fellers was flustered, and fairly taken down,
And I for a time was counted the luckiest man in town.

Once when I had a fever—I won't forget it soon—
I was hot as a basted turkey and crazy as a loon!
Never an hour went by me when she was out of sight—
She nursed me true and tender, and stuck to me day and night.

And if ever a house was tidy, and ever a kitchen clean,
Her house and kitchen was tidy as any I ever seen;
And I don't complain of Betsey, or any of her acts,
Exceptin' as when we've quarrelled, and twitted each other
on facts.

So draw up the papers, lawyer; and I'll go home tonight,
And read the agreement to her, and see if it's all right;
And then, in the mornin', I'll sell to a tradin' man I know,
And kiss the child that was left to us, and out in the world I'll go.

And one thing put in the paper, that first to me didn't occur
That when I am dead at last she bring me back to her;
And lay me under the maples I planted years ago,
When she and I was happy; before we quarrelled so.

And when she dies I wish that she would be laid by me;
And, lyin' together in silence, perhaps we might agree;
And if ever we meet in Heaven, I wouldn't think it queer
If we loved each other the better for what we quarrelled here.

Will Carleton

(How they made up follows)

How Betsey and I Made Up

Give us your hand, Mr. Lawyer: how do you do today?
You drew up that paper—I s'pose you want your pay.
Don't cut down your figures; make it an X or a V;
For that 'ere written agreement was just the makin' of me!

Goin' home that evenin' I tell you I was blue,
Thinkin' of all my troubles, and what I was goin' to do;
And if my hosses hadn't been the steadiest team alive,
They'd 've tipped me over for certain; for I couldn't see where
to drive.

No—for I was laborin' under a heavy load;
No—for I was travellin' an entirely different road;
For I was a'tracin' over the path of our lives ag'in,
And observin' where we missed the way, and where we might
have been.

And many a corner we'd turned that just to a quarrel led,
When I ought to 've held my temper, and driven straight ahead;
And the more I thought it over the more these memories came,
And the more I struck the opinion that I was the most to blame.

And things I had long forgotten kept risin' in my mind,
Of little matters betwixt us, where Betsey was good and kind;
And these things flashed all through me, as you know things
sometimes will
When a feller's alone in the darkness, and everything is still.

"But," says I, "we're too far along to take another track,
And when I put my hand to the plough I do not oft turn back;
And 'tain't an uncommon thing now for couples to smash
in two";
And so I set my teeth together, and vowed I'd see it through.

And when I come in sight o' the house 'twas some'at in the night,
And just as I turned a hill-top I see the kitchen light;

Which often a han'some pictur' to a hungry person makes,
But it don't interest a man so much that's goin' to pull up stakes.

And when I went in the house, the table was set for me—
As good a supper 's ever I saw, or ever want to see;
And I crammed the agreement down in my pocket as well as ever I could,
And fell to eatin' my victuals, which somehow didn't taste good.

And Betsey, she pretended to be lookin' all around the house;
But she watched my side coat-pocket like a cat would watch a mouse;
And then she went to foolin' a little with her cup,
And intently readin' a newspaper—a holdin' it wrong side up.

And when I'd done with my supper, I drawed the agreement out,
And give it to her without a word, for she knowed what 'twas about;
And then I hummed a little tune; but now and then a note
Got bu'sted by some animal that hopped up in my throat.

Then Betsey she went an' took her specks from off the mantelshelf,
And read the agreement over quite softly to herself;
Read it by little and little; for her eyes is gettin' old,
And lawyers' writin' ain't no point, especially when it's cold.

And after she'd read a little she give my arm a touch,
And kindly said she was afraid I was 'lowin' her too much
But when she was through she went for me, her face a-streamin' with tears,
And kissed me for the first time in half-a-dozen years!

I don't know what you'll think, Sir—I didn't come to inquire—
But I picked up that agreement and stuffed it in the fire;
And I told her we'd bury the hatchet alongside of the cow;
And we struck an agreement never to have another row.

And I told her in the future I wouldn't speak cross nor rash
If half the crockery in the house was broken all to smash;
And she said in regards to Heaven, we'd try and prove its worth.
By startin' a branch establishment, and runnin' it here on earth.

And so we sat a-talkin' three-quarters of the night,
And opened our hearts to each other until they both grew light;
And the days when I was winnin' her away from so many men
Was nothin' to that evenin' I courted her over again.

Next mornin' an ancient virgin took pains to call on us,
Her lamp all trimmed and a-burnin'—to kindle another fuss;
But when she went to pryin' 'round and openin' up old sores,
My Betsey rose politely, and showed her out-of-doors!

Since then I don't deny but we've had a word or two;
But we've got our eyes wide open now, and know just what to do
When one speaks cross the other just meets it with a laugh,
And the first one's ready to give up considerable more than half.

So make out your bill, Mr. Lawyer: don't stop short of an X;
Make it more if you want to, for I have got the checks!
I'm richer than a National Bank, with all its treasures told:
For I've got a wife at home now that's worth her weight in gold.

Will Carleton

A MANUAL
on Home and Family Living

The Home: Courtship, Marriage and Children

Dr. Rice covers almost every phase of the subject suggested by the title. In direct, spiritual language he gives what God says about the most intimate experiences of life that begin when young people come to the age of interest in the opposite sex, through courtship, marriage, the bringing of children into the world, and bringing up a family. Facts of nature, whispered and talked under the wrong environment, Dr. Rice meets face to face with wise and scriptural answers, without sidestepping the facts or dodging the issues.

Think of making an unchristian home Christian, a sad home happy, a perplexed and confused home happy and serene—a wrong home right! This book, by God's help, will do it!

THE HOME has become a handbook for homes, a manual for happy Christian living.

22 chapters, 381 large pages, hard binding, $5.50; paper binding, $1.95.

Postage and handling rates: up to $2.00, 70¢; up to $5.00, 90¢; over $5.00, 15%. Tennessee residents please add 6% sales tax.

SWORD OF THE LORD Murfreesboro, Tennessee 37130